D1384289

TRANSFORMATION:
THE MISSING PIECE

Changing Your Life,
Your Workplace,
Your Church
& Your City

Dr. D. Vincent (Bud) Ford

Streams Publishing Company

Published by Streams Publishing Company
718 Stratford Dr., Sidney, OH 45365
937-492-7633
budford@bright.net
www.dvincentford.com

All rights reserved. No part of this book may be reproduced, or transmitted in any form or by any means electronic or mechanical, including photocopying, recording or by any information storage and retrieval system, without written permission from the author, except for the inclusion of brief quotations in a review.

© 2006 by Dr. D. Vincent (Bud) Ford

ISBN: 1-933358-00-9

Library of Congress Control Number: 2005903971

Please mail any corrections for the next printing to:
Streams Publishing Co.
P.O. Box 260
Sidney, Ohio 45365

Book and Cover Design and Production
by Casa Graphics, Inc., Burbank, CA

Printed by Central Plains Book Manufacturing
Winfield, KS

DEDICATION

This book is dedicated first to my Lord and Savior Jesus Christ. The intent of this book is only to bring Him glory.

Second, this book is dedicated to my wife Marilyn, my partner, my helpmate, my encourager, my supporter, my friend and my love. Without her unwavering love, devotion, confidence, support, encouragement and help this work would not be a reality.

ACKNOWLEDGEMENTS

So many people deserve recognition for the results of this book that it is impossible to mention them all. I do desire, however, to give special recognition to a few outstanding contributors to this work.

First, I have gratefulness of heart for the team, Pastor Jim Maxwell, George Broderick and Randy Schloss, that went with me into Marion Correctional Institution (MCI) for the Experiencing God gatherings. Your willingness to walk in the presence of the Lord and your dedication to the Lord's work will have a lasting impact on many of those incarcerated, as well as on myself. Thank you for your commitment, courage and spirit.

Second, to John Beason, deceased, whose friendship I will always cherish and whose leadership helped to put MCI on the road to transformation.

Third, to the men who attended the Experiencing God gatherings, especially to a very special friend, DL, whose help and love of the Lord has been invaluable. I have learned more from all of you than you could ever imagine.

Fourth, to the City Gates core group of Dayton, Ohio, under the leadership of Bishop Truman Martin, for your friendship, your heart for seeing the city changed and your willingness to cross denominational and racial barriers to advance God's kingdom in the Miami Valley.

Fifth, I want to thank Ernie and Patty Weckbaugh of Casa Graphics, Inc. for your invaluable help and patience in seeing me through this book project.

Last, but not least, to my loving wife, Marilyn, who has stood by me through all. When I have been down, she has picked me up, dusted me off, wiped my bloody nose, given me a hug and a pat on the behind and told me to get back in the game because I could do it. I love you Marilyn.

TABLE OF CONTENTS

(CONTINUED ON NEXT PAGE)

TABLE OF CONTENTS (CONT.)

FOREWORD

Having spent many years actively involved in the prayer movement, both nationally and internationally, and today being primarily involved in spreading the message of hope to the church about the supremacy of Christ and all that Christ is, I welcome this work by Dr. D. Vincent (Bud) Ford. It has the potential of contributing significantly to biblical transformation in our nation, especially our prisons.

Listen to some of the messages Dr. Bud delivers. *"The missing piece is that Christ is all and in all, and we must submit to that truth in our entire being and in our deeds, and we must be desperately in love with Him."* He also says, *"We are the city—and we are the community. If we desire community transformation, we, by definition, must desire transformation of our selves."* Again, he says, *"We must change ourselves first so that our changed lives can affect our environment in different ways than we now affect it."* Another message: *"If we are not desperately in love with Jesus Christ and if we are not in His presence, the strategies, plans and efforts will be coming from our own strength and we will fail, or at best have only human results, and we cannot expect to have supernatural, God results."*

Dr. Bud is speaking my heart. I believe the greatest crisis of our time in America is within the church: it is Christians who need to be re-awakened to Jesus Christ as Lord—what I call the "Supremacy of Christ." To be sure, we often settle for allowing Him to be *central* in our lives, by allowing Him to be the *center* of who WE are, where WE are headed, what WE are doing and how WE are blessed. This is important and necessary, but there is much more to how we need to be viewing Christ.

The great crisis in the church today is that we do not respond to Him as though we understood what it means when we say that Christ is *supreme*. Recognizing Christ as supreme means recognizing that it is He who keeps us at the center of who HE is, of where HE is headed, of what HE is doing and of how HE is blessed. That is the difference between the "centrality of Christ" and the "supremacy of Christ."

Dr. Bud emphasizes, if we do not hold Christ supreme in our life, then we must hold someone else supreme. That someone else is usually ourselves, and that just will not work. We move in our own strength and, in many cases, do not even realize it.

What you will receive from this book is a fascinating look at how God has sovereignly intervened in a men's prison, radically transforming its environment. You will also receive a look at the principles involved. Here is wisdom to apply those principles to your life, your church and your city.

In this book, you will read powerful testimonies from inmates involved in the move of God at their prison. You will learn the different ways the missing piece of Christ's supremacy has manifested itself in the prison.

Dr. Bud has skillfully and uniquely undergirded principles behind the model of a transformed prison with God's Word about coming into His presence, His message to the church, His teaching on prayer, faith and living in a Christlike way. He points to the need for balance between being in the presence of the Lord and doing His work. Again, he speaks my heart. Being in His presence and spending *heart* time with Him is the only way we will internalize Him for all that He is—in His full supremacy—and thus live for Him as He deserves.

Here is a quick overview:

In part one Dr. Bud covers God's model seen at the Marion Correctional Institution.

In part two he explores the pattern God has provided for us to come into His presence as well as the prayer, faith and lifestyle needed to stay in His presence. This is not just for Christians in prison; these insights can help all of us.

In part three Dr. Bud draws upon his vast years of experience to deal with issues of concern to those responsible for leadership of movements to change churches and cities. This part deals with issues in city reaching movements, and concerns of group growth and group dynamics.

In part four he deals with the state of the church today and looks closely at Christ's message to the churches in our current day. Part four also conveniently summarizes principles from throughout the book and looks at where we might go next.

After nearly twenty years of effort in America to transform cities we often see only minimal results. It is difficult to know what a transformed city might look like in our country. According to Dr. Bud, we have a model of what it might look like from—of all places—the men's prison of Marion Correctional Institution.

The key question that must be asked is "Are the results of Marion Correctional Institution reproducible in a church or city?" Many other prisons have tried to obtain the results of Marion Correctional Institution with little success. However, according to Dr. Bud, the programs and strategies are not the key. Rather the advance of the Kingdom in Marion Correctional Institution is to be found in the heart of those at the center of the movement. The leaders are desperately in love with Jesus and live with the understanding that He is *supreme*. Many of the inmates freely communicate the supremacy of Jesus Christ. As that message spreads, more and more people are becoming passionate for Christ.

So again the question, "Are the results of Marion Correctional Institution reproducible?" Dr. Bud would answer with an unequivocal and resounding "Yes!" but again not through programs, systems or strategies. Rather we must understand the Supremacy of Christ, learn to come into His presence and be desperately in love with Him. It is from there that He will send us to do His work.

Do I concur with what Dr. Bud has stated? Absolutely. This is exactly to what I have dedicated my own life: the proclamation of the supremacy of God's Son everywhere, in our churches, in our cities, in our prison, too.

Dr. Bud is committed to serving the church by revitalizing our hope about the transformation of our communities. This book is a testimony to that fact.

David Bryant
2005

Author of: *Christ Is All: A Joyful Manifesto on the Supremacy of God's Son,* and many other books.

Founder, *PROCLAIM HOPE* (previously called *Concerts of Prayer International*).

INTRODUCTION

Are you hungry to see your city transformed?

Are you tired of the lack of progress over the past twenty years to transform cities in America?

Are you ready to gain wisdom on how to reach your city for Christ?

Are you looking for application—rather than theory?

Are you ready to do what it takes to see transformation take place in yourself and the lives of people around you?

Are you ready to see your church transformed and become a dwelling place for the Lord?

Are you ready to see darkness pushed back and the Kingdom of God advanced to transform your city?

Are you looking for city transformation finally to happen in America? This book gives great encouragement and hope for that to happen.

Do you want to know what has been missing?

If so, this book is for you.

This book is about the missing piece. God has provided that piece for us in a way we can see, understand and apply. It shows us what transformation looks like in America.

It will transform your life and your city. *God has revealed the missing piece for America in the most unlikely place—a prison.*

That missing piece is transferable to your life, your church, your workplace or school and to your city.

In this book, you will discover the missing piece in transformation and learn how to:

◆ Change your city to reflect the Kingdom of God.

◆ Take control of how God's model is able to TRANSFORM your LIFE, your CHURCH and your CITY.

◆ Revolutionize how you approach life.

◆ Apply the lessons from a TRANSFORMED prison in America.

◆ Build a sacred dwelling place for God's presence.
◆ See the difference between "being in God's presence" and "doing God's work."
◆ Lead your church into intimacy with God.
◆ Develop a true and authentic relationship with God.
◆ Understand the meaning of Christ's message to the church.
◆ Succeed in following the patterns God has provided to you for transforming your cities.
◆ Apply God's principles to change your city.

This book is about being in God's presence first, and learning to stay there, before He sends us to do His work. When we combine learning to be in His presence with what we already know about developing the strategies for doing His work, we get the complete picture for transforming our cities. *We must learn that there has to be a balance—and that the balance must be maintained over time—between being in His presence (and all that entails) and being sent to work by Him.* This is what has been missing in America; I believe this is the reason we have not seen transformed cities.

God has provided a model for us in America so we can see what it looks like, and what is required of us, for bringing transformation. That model of transformation is seen in a men's state prison in Ohio.

Some may think we have nothing to learn from a prison, but it has been transformed and our cities have not. This book shows that God has used the most unlikely place to teach us some very fundamental lessons about who is in charge.

The book is divided into four parts. The FIRST PART covers the model God has provided us, as well as testimonies of truly transformed men living in a small transformed community of about 2,300 people in the prison setting. The missing piece for transformation is looked at from the perspective of the success it has had in the lives of inmates and in the community of the prison.

The SECOND PART covers the pattern God has provided

for us to come into His presence. It also covers patterns of lifestyle and faith we must learn to follow, not just know and acknowledge in our heads.

The THIRD PART represents a change of pace in the book and deals with issues of concern mainly to those responsible for leadership of a group, or of a city-reaching movement. Organizational concerns are addressed here. Likewise, the delicate concerns of dealing with group growth and group dynamics are dealt with. Similarly, we cover the sensitive dynamics of understanding, and dealing with, the different types of power and influence used by people.

Busy people, who can only involve themselves in city-reaching efforts on a part-time basis, could skip quickly over this third part without missing the flow or purpose of the book.

The FOURTH PART deals with the state of the church today by looking at Christ's message to the church. It also summarizes where we have been in our journey through the book and where we might go next.

After twenty years of attempting to transform cities in America with just minimal success, we need to acknowledge that what we have been doing has had something missing—it has not worked well. ***There is wisdom in this book and I believe it touches the nerve of what has been missing in our efforts at reaching cities.***

My prayer is that God will be glorified by this work and that it will fall into the hands of those God has been preparing to receive its message.

Psalm 25:9 (NLT)
> *He leads the humble in what is right, teaching them his way.*

PART 1
THE MODEL

Introduction to Part 1

Part one introduces the Marion Correctional Institution (MCI) model of transformation. This model was revealed by events leading up to, and including, the move of God at the prison. Since the MCI prison represents a small city, the MCI model of transformation gives us a picture of what a changed city can look like in America. The model also reveals the missing piece to transforming our cities in America.

The comments and testimonies by inmates reveal expectation and fervor in their lives and attitudes, which comes from being in the presence of the Lord.

The missing piece is expressed in many different manifestations in Part One. *That missing piece represents the absolute necessity of our first being in the presence of the Lord before He can send us to do His work, and it involves learning to remain in His presence while doing His work.*

Luke 4:18-19 (NLT)

"The Spirit of the Lord is upon me, for he has appointed me to preach Good News to the poor. He has sent me to proclaim that captives will be released, that the blind will see, that the downtrodden will be freed from their oppressors, [19]and that the time of the Lord's favor has come."

MARION CORRECTIONAL INSTITUTION

MARION CORRECTIONAL INSTITUTION (MCI)

It is just like God to use the most unexpected place as a model for what many believe He desires to do in America. Eight years ago, the State of Ohio men's prison, Marion Correctional Institution (MCI), was a very dark and dangerous place; today it is a place where many of the inmates are at various stages of being personally transformed by God. There is no question that God is moving in a very special and powerful way at this prison. What has happened there is nothing short of miraculous and something only God could do.

If we want more peace and righteousness in our own lives, in our homes, in our churches, and in our cities, then we must have less sin and evil in each of these places. The concept is simple: the more peace and righteousness we have, the less sin and evil predominates; the inverse is also true: the more sin and evil that exists in a place, the less peace and righteousness exist there.

This is an easy concept to put into words, but implementing the concept is much more difficult. Let us explore what more peace and righteousness looks like in the difficult prison environment of MCI.

Eight years ago, there was well over an average of 1,000 incident reports each month reflecting numerous violent occurrences. Today, there are fewer than a dozen such reports filed per month. In 1996 there were 350 backlogged union grievances, compared to no backlog today. This represents a drastic transformation.

According to Christine Money, warden of the Marion Correctional Institution, the environment of the prison changes when incarcerated men find hope, forgiveness and healing, and the impact at MCI can be seen through a very low rate of rule violations, inmate grievances and other serious incidents.[1] Many of those incarcerated in Ohio prisons today know of MCI as the "Christian" prison and as the place where many Christian faith-based programs are taking place.

Eight years ago, the violent Aryan Brotherhood gang involved itself deeply in criminal activity and was one of the predominate gangs in the prison. Today the Aryan Brotherhood gang at MCI has been essentially dismantled and deactivated because of the gang leader, John Beason, receiving Jesus Christ as his Lord and Savior.

You will read more about John later in this chapter as an important stream flowing together with other streams to change MCI, and you will find his story in Chapter 2.

Eight years ago, 15 percent of inmates tested positive for drugs. Today it is less than one percent.

Eight years ago, it was hardly safe to walk down the halls at MCI. Today you will see men carrying their Bibles with them as they move through the halls, greeting one another with heartfelt greetings, and most astounding of all, you will see men on their knees praying in their dorms and cell-locks.[2]

Eight years ago, it was not macho—or safe—to cry, hug or show emotion; these all happen today on a regular basis.

Eight years ago, it was unheard of for people to accept the Lord as their personal Savior. Today it happens on a regular basis.

Eight years ago, it was difficult to find a Bible study. Today, Bible studies are abundant.

VISION

Five years ago, I had a vivid vision where I saw a large mass of men gathered together out in the yard at MCI. The men had their hands raised in the air singing and praising the Lord. Some of the men were on their knees and some of them were lying on the ground worshiping the Lord; while others were standing in small groups with their arms around each other praying, singing and praising God.

There was an opportunity for me to reveal this vision to the warden and to let her know she needed to get herself and the prison ready, because revival was coming to MCI. The warden very bluntly responded, "No way, the rules don't permit anything like that here!" That was in the year 2000.

The summer of 2003 and during the summer of 2004, the warden and I both had the awesome privilege of seeing that vision fulfilled. We were able to stand in, and walk live in, the middle of that vision. When Promise Keepers (PK) came *live* to MCI with their stadium event, during the summers of 2003 and 2004, the warden and I were both able to look out over the crowd in the same yard that had appeared in the vision. That vision was fulfilled right before our very eyes; we saw exactly what God had shown in the vision.

Tom Fortson, president of Promise Keepers, spoke at the 2004 event and said, "Everywhere I go, people are talking about MCI."

Having a live PK event at MCI was unheard of and an unprecedented experience. Here, many inmates committed their lives to the Lord. There were over one hundred salvations in 2003 and during the altar call at the 2004 event, over half of the 1,000 inmates stood to make either a first time commitment, or a rededication of their lives to the Lord.

The words of one of the correction officers at MCI are very revealing about the changes that have taken place within this prison. He said that *MCI used to be a very scary, spooky place, especially at night; but now that was gone and there was a real peace in the areas where he worked.*

It was mentioned before that if we want more peace and righteousness in our lives, in our homes and in our cities, then sin and evil in those places must decrease. What you have seen from MCI, and what you will see throughout this book, is a picture of what it looks like when sin and evil decrease, and when peace and righteousness increase as it has at MCI.

To be holy is to be consecrated to the Lord, it is being completely set apart and separated from the imperfection and the impurity of the world, it is being different from the world. *Many of the inmates at MCI are holy, and as their peace and righteousness increases and spreads to others in the prison, sin and evil decrease.* We need holiness, peace and righteousness to happen in our own lives and in our cities.

ABOUT MCI

MCI is a men's prison with a population of 1,823 inmates and 487 staff members, of which 282 are security staff. MCI is a security level 1 & 2 prison, which means it can house maximum and medium security level inmates, and it has an annual budget of $37,458,408 with an annual cost per inmate of $20,103.25 and a daily cost per inmate of $55.08. The prison opened in 1954.

Numerous rehabilitation programs have been available at the prison for many years; these include industries, community service, vocational and academic programs.

MCI has some unique secular programs available to the inmates. Among these are:

Prison News Network (PNN): PNN is involved with

producing many video programs at MCI and utilizes digital cameras and equipment with the capability of producing professional quality videos. PNN focuses on inmate programs, training videos for departments, community service projects, and special projects for the Department of Rehabilitation and Correction.

My Child & I: The program is designed to increase an offender's awareness of responsibility to the family through positive nurturing and interaction. Approximately 30 inmates go through a screening process and attend parenting skills classes prior to the event. Volunteers from MCI and outside organizations and churches assist in numerous areas during the program. The families are able to play games, produce family videos, decide on choices about what crafts to make, read to each other or listen to the storyteller, experience the adventures of the Center of Science and Industry, pet and hold animals from the wildlife center and the MCI farm. Each family receives a birthday cake and ice cream, along with a birthday goodie bag, to celebrate birthdays missed. The program has been very successful and well received by inmates and their families.

Life Line: This is a program provided to prepare inmates for a successful reentry to their community. Life Line is an industrial computer-training program for inmates aimed at providing exposure to computers and technology. The program serves up to 900 men annually.

A Better Way: This is a program directed at troubled youth, and it is intended to guide them toward an awareness of the consequences of the choices and decisions they make in their lives. MCI inmates currently provide this program at the nearby Marion County Juvenile Correctional Facility.

Assistance with Discovering Alternative Problem-Solutions Together (ADAPT): This is a voluntary process available to inmates involved in a dispute to discuss and explore problem solutions.

Fathers Reaching Out: This is a program designed to build upon and enhance relationships between incarcerated fathers and their children. This is done by providing educationally based interactive learning materials for incarcerated fathers.

These unique secular programs are all in addition to the secular programs of anger management, conflict management, AA, drug rehabilitation, support group classes, and numerous other programs and classes.

DEPARTMENT OF REHABILITATION AND CORRECTIONS

The Director of The Ohio Department of Rehabilitation and Corrections, Reginald Wilkinson, had the following to say about rehabilitation and corrections in Ohio and about MCI.[3]

> "Through the Reentry Initiative we are addressing the further expansion of such linkages across the state. One key area of focus is the development of a statewide strategy for engaging faith communities throughout Ohio in reentry. The intent is to establish viable connecting points across the prison-community divide, relative to reentry; from the sentencing and admission to the prison system, through the confinement, to the release under supervision in the community. An Inter-Denominational Faith Council has recently been established that will cover the northern, central and southern regions of the state. The regional councils will interact with the institutions and parole officers in their particular geographic areas to provide resources, mentoring, and structure to offenders returning home.
>
> The commitment to faith-based participation in Ohio corrections is uniquely positioned to draw on impressive efforts that

are already underway in Marion Correctional Institution (MCI) that center on spiritual growth and positive community living."

The purpose of telling about the secular and faith-based programs is to stress that prisons in Ohio are involved in faith-based programs, including Kairos, which will be discussed in more detail later. In addition, it is important to note that Warden Money was warden at another prison that had the Kairos programs, but that prison did not experience the kind of change that MCI has experienced. *Also, note that while the programs at MCI have been used as models for other prisons to copy, there are few, if any, of the other prisons experiencing the movement of God as MCI is experiencing it; few, if any, have been transformed as MCI has been transformed as a result of using MCI's programs.*

THE MCI MODEL

It is important to note that MCI is not the model itself; MCI represents an example, a picture of God's pattern, being carried out in life. *God's pattern is the true model and MCI is a demonstration of that pattern. We cannot copy MCI, but we can see how MCI has lived out God's pattern so we can learn from that basic picture.*

An overall description of what I have come to call the MCI Model would be something like the following: Unassociated activities and events began to take place in unrelated ways. None of the people involved in the activities or events were looking for each other, or looking to network. The need of the inmates for God's presence, the need for a sense of self-worth and hope, and the need for survival in a difficult environment was driving what was taking place with the inmates.

What was happening at MCI was also driven by the revelation given to the warden on a Walk to Emmaus weekend retreat. It was there she realized that the unconditional agape love and acceptance by God could change the lives of many inmates and give them hope.

What was taking place at MCI was not driven by a desire for good control of violent incident statistics to be used on state reports, for a transformed environment, or for impressive résumés—in short, what was happening was not for selfish or for the wrong motives.

What God began to reveal at MCI was a number of different streams beginning to flow and beginning to come together in a river. About four years ago, I would say that the river was just beginning to flow about ankle deep.

Streams coming together is symbolic language to portray, especially in the spiritual realm, what God was doing. The streams represented different people's activity that God was directing, often without them even knowing it.

City Reach International, on the home page of their web site,[4] states that there is an expectation by believers everywhere that God is intending a major move of His Spirit in our nation and around the world. They, at City Reach International, are convinced His visitation is intended to transform the religious, social, economic and political structures of our culture and spark an awakening and response among the unsaved in unprecedented proportions. They state that the uncertainty regarding this grand expectation is neither in God's willingness nor in His ability to do it, but in the church's readiness to receive it and effectively steward it.

I believe City Reach International is correct in their assessment, and *I believe God has provided the picture through the MCI model—without the intentional effort of man—to show us the absolute necessity of getting the true church, the Body of Christ, ready to receive the move of God described and to effectively steward that move.*

I believe God has demonstrated His grace to us by presenting us with a picture of His power in the most unlikely setting of a prison. He has shown us this picture so that we, as His Body, would take seriously this necessity of getting the church ready.

I will describe some of the different streams, as I understand them, and how they began to flow together to form the river now flowing at MCI. The flow of this river is the work of the Holy Spirit, and it represents the model God has provided for us to study and adapt to our city transformation efforts.

We need to draw concepts from what we learn from how the streams flow together, but we must also be careful we do not try to duplicate any particular stream or combination of streams. The picture God has given us represents a conceptual model to be applied to our own lives and cities and not an exact model to duplicate.

We will now identify some of the different streams at MCI.

STREAMS

The Stream of the Ministry of Theater: I believe this was the first stream. It has been in operation for seventeen years, and it was started by one of the previous chaplains. As of March 2005, there have been 37 productions, and the most recent productions have each hosted over 1,600 outside visitors to the performances.

One thing the Ministry of Theater contributed that started it flowing as an early stream was to focus on religious themes at Easter and Christmas. Even though there was no evangelistic thrust to the Theater, it has continued to provide an open door for the Holy Spirit to begin to penetrate some lives and provide some light in the darkness of the prison.

The inmates write the script, score the music and make most of the costumes and scenery. The programs have a religious context and the quality is outstanding. The performances are open to the public and free of charge.

There was no intention of this program leading to revival or any transformation of the prison. Its purpose was to serve as a creative outlet for those participating; however, it has played a role in softening the ground for expectations to increase and to provide an avenue for involvement with other Christians and involvement in

Christian activities.

The Stream of Intercessors: In the early 1990s a small group of inmates began to pray together. It started with only five men, and they could only meet in groups of three at a time because of prison security regulations. They prayed for revival, for light to come into that dark place, for more Christians and for Bible study opportunities.

This group of early prayer warriors plowed ground for others who would follow later. Intercessory prayer groups began to spring up, and today there are a number of groups of fervent, dedicated prayer warriors. God has also opened a way for them to be able to engage in Bible studies. Some of the original prayer warriors are still at MCI serving life terms, and they have become strong Christian mentors for others.

The Stream of a New Warden: In 1996 Warden Money came to MCI from serving as warden at Marysville Ohio Reformatory for Women (ORW). She had served at ORW for a number of years. Warden Money did not want to come to MCI because of its reputation as a violent and crime-infested prison; however, God had different plans.

Warden Money is a Christian, and while at ORW she participated in a Christian weekend retreat called "The Walk to Emmaus." From the experience she had, she knew that the unity and unconditional agape love demonstrated on that weekend retreat had to get into the prison because it could provide real hope for inmates.

There is a Christian organization called "Kairos" that offers the same kind of weekend as the Walk to Emmaus weekend offers, only in the prisons. Warden Money arranged to bring Kairos into ORW to share the Christian love of Christ with the women inmates.

It is worth noting here that revival, or the movement of God, as has been seen at MCI, did not take place at ORW even though Kairos and Warden Money were there.

When Warden Money came to MCI, she also made sure the Kairos program was brought there. She began to make other changes as well, and a number of the changes created channels for new streams to begin to flow.

The Stream of New Personnel: As some key employees left the institution, it just seemed that God sent people who were Christian or sympathetic toward Christianity to fill those positions. God has worked through employees who have come with different mindsets and with different attitudes from that of the old guard. There is a prison mentality made up of control, coercion and punishment. When that mentality begins to be replaced with the mentality of hating the sin but loving the sinner and of seeing the sinner as God sees him, then that change in mindset leads to a completely different environmental climate.

It must be noted that not all employees have the new mindset, but it appears that those who do are growing in number.

Any good leader will pay close attention to institutional morale and institutional climate—or atmosphere, and Warden Money is a good leader. However, there are many good leaders in the prison system, but other prisons have not experienced a move of God as MCI has just because of having good leadership. We need to keep following these streams to begin to see how God has worked.

Incidentally, if anyone thinks they can implement a man-made program or process which will lead to an outpouring of the Holy Spirit, they are in error. All we can do is submit totally to God, be obedient and stay in His presence. When we are in His presence and able to hear His voice and we put into action what He is speaking, then God will do what has been His will from the beginning in answer to our prayers.

The Stream of Kairos: In 1997, Warden Money arranged for the Christian organization of Kairos to come into MCI to put on their weekend retreat. This has proven to be an important stream that the Lord has used. Kairos generally puts on two weekend retreats a year at MCI.

The mission of the Kairos Prison Ministry is to bring Christ's love and forgiveness to all incarcerated individuals, to their families and to those who work with them, and to assist in the transition of becoming productive citizens.

Well-trained and well-organized volunteer teams present the three-and-one-half-day weekend program that is a short course on Christianity within the prison setting. It offers a total introductive immersion to living in the Christian community. After completing the weekend, the participants are offered the opportunity to participate in weekly share and prayer groups with other inmates, monthly reunions with outside volunteers and semiannual inmate instructional retreats. The purpose of Kairos is to establish strong Christian communities among the populations of correctional institutions.

The Kairos weekend is a powerful spiritual experience, and many men have accepted Christ as their Savior during that time. Even those men who do not accept Christ as their Savior are able to experience unconditional love that is overwhelming for many of them and opens the door for their being receptive to things of God; this allows them to be receptive to the Holy Spirit working in them. For many of the inmates it is the first time in their life they have experienced that kind of overwhelming agape love. It is a life-changing event for most of the men who are able to participate in the weekend.

The weekend retreat can only accommodate 42 inmates at a time and is in high demand, so there is a large waiting list.

The Stream of Kairos Outside: This Christian ministry enables female family members of inmates to participate in a weekend spiritual renewal/retreat at the MCI Interfaith Chapel inside the prison. These family members "do time" right along with their loved ones at MCI.

During the weekend, in a safe environment with loving people, women interact with other women who are in similar situations. They learn to form small groups to support one another which gives them strength for the challenges they face.

The program serves to bring healing, reconciliation and forgiveness to the lives of participants and their families. A team of Kairos volunteers share talks and facilitate discussions that help the participants explore their relationship with God and their families.

The Stream of Kairos Torch, which is under the Kairos Prison Ministry, offers an innovative program for youthful male offenders (from 18 to 25 years of age) early in their term of incarceration. The program begins with a two-and-one-half-day weekend of structured activities and talks focusing on God's unconditional love and acceptance. After completing the weekend, the participants are given the opportunity to share weekly with a mentor, attend weekly small share and prayer groups with the Kairos community, attend monthly Kairos reunions, and attend Kairos Torch reunions every three months.

The Stream of Horizon Interfaith: Kairos graduates join with Jewish and Muslim inmates and live together for 10 months in community. A dorm at MCI is set apart and called the Horizon dorm; the living area is partitioned into separate living quarters for six inmates each. They practice their own faith, learn to live together, have planned religious studies and learn about others. It is an exciting approach to developing tolerance and respect for others. It also requires a serious adjustment for many.

The Stream of Outside Brothers: Operating as a branch program of Kairos, men outside the prison from the Kairos community are assigned to act as mentors to individual inmates who have gone through the Kairos weekend. The two of them meet together each week for ten months. The inmates consistently rate this particular stream their most well-liked program. For many of the inmates this is one of the first times in their lives that someone gives genuine, positive, caring attention to them.

This particular stream has had a profound impact on changing the spiritual climate at MCI. The close relationship that develops between the inmate and his Christian mentor and the accountability factor of the inmate to the mentor is powerful. The mentor will often ask the inmate how it went the previous week when a Christian response was given to a particular situation he faced during the week.

As it is turning out, many of the inmates are growing

in their spiritual maturity so rapidly that they end up mentoring many of the mentors.

The Stream of Promise Keepers: We discussed PK earlier, but it deserves mention here as an important stream used by God. PK has offered a weekly opportunity for inmates to attend a non-threatening Christian event. The weekly rally is a safe place to attend for those who are curious, and at the same time, the weekly message has opened the door for many to receive the Lord.

The Stream of Silent Choir: This is a group of Christian inmates consisting of about eighty men. While the audience hears the music and words from a recording, in unison the men "sign" the words; it has a powerful and an emotional impact. The silent choir has turned out to be a showcase for the prison. The Warden initiated and encouraged the men in the silent choir; now inmates lead the choir themselves. This group performs for almost all special activities taking place at the prison.

Members of this group are hand selected from the Christian population, and it is an honor and privilege to be a part of it. It provides a real incentive for Christian inmates to work toward selection for participation because of the special privileges of being a part of most of the activities that take place in the institution where there are outside visitors. It also keeps men active in their faith.

The Stream of Communication to the prison population flows out of the Prison News Network (PNN) department. While much of the communication has been secular, more Christian programming and information continues to be added. "Men of Faith," a production of PNN, is broadcast throughout the prison. It is focused on the inmates themselves. Many testimonies, as well as conversations between inmates, dealing with their own faith and with the issues they may have in maintaining their faith in the prison atmosphere are frequently used in productions. The topics are raw, gut level, down to earth, no holds barred issues on living their faith. This program is the highest-rated television program from PNN—even above movies and sports programs. The men want to hear about the faith of others and their individual struggles in their faith walk. Representatives from all the different faiths in the institution are given an opportunity to express themselves.

The Stream of Volunteer Programs: The chaplain's office oversees more than 500 volunteers who provide many other Christ centered or faith-based programs at MCI. Without elaborating, I will just mention a few such programs: Discipleship study groups, quiet meditation, basic theology class, many different Bible study groups, Experiencing God class, Experiencing God retreat, Catholic study groups and the prison Alpha course to name just a few. There are also numerous religious programs meeting the needs of the Muslim, Jewish, and Hispanic populations.

The Stream of John Beason: He was an individual who was a vital stream that God released in the early years of the transformation of MCI. The next chapter is devoted to an interview with John and the interview is written in his own words. *His key role was that of leader of the violent Aryan Brotherhood gang, but he gave his life to Christ and turned the gang around from violence, sin and crime, to that of serving the Lord.* He also reconciled with other prison gangs such as the Bloods, the Crips and the Latino Kings. John is directly responsible for hundreds of inmates coming to the Lord, and indirectly, for hundreds more

While the role John played is important to the early transformation of MCI, it must be noted that there are hundreds of other individual and group stories of those whom God worked through over the years to bring the change at MCI.

Summary of the Streams: It was mentioned that the MCI Model was conceptual. Following are some concepts that may be gleaned from the different streams.

First, none of the streams was looking for ways to transform MCI and make it a Christian Prison.

Second, the streams were independent activities, people or groups. Those different streams wanted to have hope, and wanted to bring hope, as well as bring the presence of Christ.

Third, somehow, they seemed to know intuitively that for safety, peace and righteousness all to exist, the sin, violence and evil had to decrease.

Fourth, there was no big plan or strategy to bring about safety, peace or righteousness across the institution. The change that has taken place has been based on coming into the presence of God and seeking His direction on meeting immediate needs that existed.

Fifth, those inmates involved in the streams seemed to know instinctively that how they had lived their lives had gotten them nowhere; therefore, they were willing to turn their lives over to God, to seek His face and to come into His presence.

Sixth, just as at MCI, we know that many different and unrelated streams currently exist in a city; however, they are not connected. Most do not know the others exist, and they do not know how to find each other even when they suspect other streams are out there.

Lastly, we can see the reality of the concept that we are, in fact, all part of the Body of Christ, and that we bring different talents and usefulness to the whole. We see here just what that concept looks like, rather than simply giving it lip service. *When different gangs like the Aryan Brotherhood, the Bloods, the Crips and the Latino Kings can reconcile and work toward the good of all, why is it so difficult for the different churches, races, interest groups and associations to unite for the benefit of the whole city?*

How did all this happen at MCI? It did not happen at the other prison where the warden was assigned; it has not happened at other prisons that have the Kairos program; it has not happened at other prisons that have tried to copy what MCI has done; it has not happened at other prisons that have religious programs. It was God. His grace has given us a working model of how it looks when we allow God to work, and when we learn to come into His presence, to hear His voice and to be obedient.

It did not happen with a big plan or strategy to change

the institution. It did not happen based on the plans or strategies of individuals or groups to fulfill some grand vision for revival. *It happened with an intentional effort to bring hope to, and change the individual. That effort involved learning to relate to one another and learning to apply biblical principles in everyday life in the prison. God was involved in reaching each of those individuals. It was something that grew out of each individual allowing God to change his heart.*

In the next chapter, we will hear from John Beason, and in the chapter following that we will hear from other inmates.

THE MODEL AND THE PATTERN

I have referred to the MCI model thus far and have indicated it is a conceptual model from which we may draw concepts that are transferable to transforming cities.

Referring to a model has been a convenient way to present the material in this book; however, note again in preparation for Part II of this book, that the real model is God's provided pattern, and not that of MCI.

MCI is but a picture example of the true model God gives us to come into His presence.

When we learn to get the pattern right, the Glory of God will fall on us and on our city. We will learn more about the pattern in Part II.

2 Chronicles 7:14 (NLT)
Then if my people who are called by my name will humble themselves and pray and seek my face and turn from their wicked ways, I will hear from heaven and will forgive their sins and heal their land.

INTERVIEW WITH JOHN BEASON

BACKGROUND

What follows is a unique interview. It is between the author (**BF**) and **John Beason**, who was the second highest-ranking officer of the Aryan Brotherhood prison gang in the State of Ohio prison system.

I had the privilege of leading John to the Lord on a Kairos weekend at Marion Correctional Institution in 1999, and then of becoming his mentor.

I would like to give you some background on why this is such an important interview.

John was mentioned briefly in the first chapter as one of the key early streams that was flowing in Marion Correctional Institution.

John received parole November 13, 2001. Because of his tremendous love for those who were the outcasts of this world, he placed his parole in jeopardy in order to witness to those people in Cleveland, Ohio. I continued to be John's spiritual mentor and we stayed in contact by phone and personal visits during his parole. I know without question that John was not involved in any criminal activity, but because of his pressing call to witness to the hurting people in this world, John was arrested for a parole violation and sent back to prison in November of 2004.

John was completely exonerated from any wrongdoing. However, because John was a parolee, there was a process that had to be followed before he could be released from prison and placed back on parole; John was waiting out that process in the Ohio State prison of Belmont Correctional Institution.

During John's years as a gang leader in the prison systems, he received many tattoos. Unsanitary needles were used to do the tattooing and John contacted hepatitis C. While he was back in prison, he could not get the medication he required.

John became ill while at Belmont and on February 5, 2005 he died in his bed. What a tragic loss for us, but John is now with the Lord and completely healed.

This interview is most likely the closest we will come to getting John's testimony about his involvement with the transformation at Marion Correctional Institution.

A second reason John's interview is so important is that, at this time, it is not possible to get an interview with the warden of Marion Correctional Institution that could be used for general public distribution. Because of what could result in potential time-consuming and costly legal entanglements, the warden's story will not be available for wide public distribution and will have to wait for her retirement.

In the following interview, there has been no attempt to edit or correct John's conversation. This is done so you may get the flavor of his impact at Marion Correctional Institution (MCI) and also of who he was as a person. This chapter is a script of a taped interview done June 18, 2004 in Cleveland, Ohio with John.

John did not want his name to be concealed as the person giving this interview, so his correct name is being used. In the next chapter, for reasons of security, I have concealed the identity of those inmates giving testimony.

INTERVIEW
Bud Ford (BF)

"Here is the gist of what this book is about John, and you can adjust your comments accordingly.

"What is clear at MCI is that Warden Money has been acting as a coordinator, arranging events in a proper and harmonious way. She has done this by acting as a facilitator, by making activities easier, by moving events forward toward completion and by assisting where needed for progress to be made. She is the one that has made changes possible institutionally.

"What has happened at MCI did not happen at the Marysville prison, even though she was the warden there, and even though the Kairos ministry was operating there.

"What the warden has been able to do at MCI is to make it possible for many different streams to begin to flow and connect to other streams. However, there was another ingredient, and that was the hand of God leading her. In addition, John, you were an important ingredient in those early days. You were one used by God at that particular season to get the streams of transformation at MCI flowing together inside the prison.

"The warden had to have someone on the inside with the inmates, to exert influence. Without your influence and God working through you in the early stages inside the prison, it is not sure how rapidly all the change would have taken place. It took her networking on the outside and you, with the heartbeat of the prison, networking on the inside.

"*Therefore, when other prison wardens and officials attempted to replicate the success of MCI, they were not able to replicate the heart of the warden or the heart of you on the inside.* God chose the warden's heart and your heart to be at the center of the MCI model, and it certainly would be helpful to have a replication of those hearts for transforming a city. In moving around

Dayton, Ohio, I have been searching for kingdom people, and my prayers have been for the Lord to identify the warden and the John Beason for that area.

"It would seem we need to identify two people or two groups of people. One group needs to have the influence to coordinate resources in the city and network diplomatically between church, ministry, government and business leaders and the other group needs to have influence on the heartbeat of the city—the needs and the pain of the city.

"Therefore, in this interview we will be looking for some clues that will help identify the character of the group or persons we need to be looking for to help transformation take place in our cities."

John Beason

"God had been working on me before the Kairos weekend. I was at the lowest point in my life; I couldn't have been worse. I was done. The thing about being like that is you don't have anything to lose. Anything other than what I was feeling at that time was a plus for me.

"I had just had a real bad situation—my mother had just passed. I had come out of another situation with the assaults on officers charged against me. I had just been to the parole board and had probably missed my chance to ever be able to go home. They gave me another 11 years, and I felt like I had missed my chance with my wife, and at that point you could have never made me believe I would ever get out of prison.

"That is where I was at; that was my frame of mind. Kairos tries to disciple men and get leaders to the weekend that can influence the other inmates; they target those individuals. That is what Christ did. He spent time with the disciples and taught them. They were just like the guys in prison; they were from all walks of life.

"The conspiracy was already put in place by the warden to get me into Kairos. She recognized that she had to have that person by her side that would cause everybody to say, 'Let's watch and see.' For me to take you into my world at the prison, everybody is going to watch and wait for me to say you are all right and can be trusted. That is the kind of world it is in there. She knew that, so she targeted me. She went so far as to get into the heads of some of the Aryan Brothers and get them into Kairos. She knew that if any of the Aryan Brothers invited me, I would have to consider it. She sent a key brother of mine to invite me. I am sure she didn't know how low I was or what I was feeling.

"The warden sent that Aryan Brother to ask me to go on the Kairos weekend. I remember times when I was in trouble and someone would pull a knife or a gun on me and I would be in a real bad spot and how I would always say, "Oh God get me out of this!" I knew who God was and I believed there was a God. My problem was that I had done so much bad in my life and I had become so good at it, that I didn't believe God had a place for me in His Kingdom. That was the lie that was fed to me by Satan and I believed it.

"I remember going into that Kairos meeting room on Thursday and there were guys there I had tried to kill and who had tried to kill me. There were homosexuals there; there were people there I would absolutely have nothing to do with under any circumstances and I remember the little prayer I said, 'God, I really don't know why I'm here, but if this is what you got for me then give me some peace.' Before, anytime I got in a situation, I would reach out for God, and as soon as He got me out of that mess I was off and running on my own. I never took time to hear Him; I never honored Him; I never heard what He said. I didn't know how to hear Him; I wouldn't slow down enough. Because of who I was in the Aryan Brotherhood, I had to watch everybody. I didn't know who it was going to be or when it was going to happen, but I knew it would come and someone would try to kill me; I would have been a big feather in their cap.

"So because of that, I was always one of the last guys to go to sleep and one of the first to wake up. I went up to the dorm that night and it was a mad house: guys shouting, radios blaring, TV blasting, guys fighting; and I went up to all that and God gave me what I had asked. He gave me peace; I lay down in all that chaos and I went to sleep. It was the first time in 20 years that I had gotten a good nights sleep and peace.

"I got up the next morning and I had not intended to go back to Kairos, but then I wanted to go—something had changed. I wanted to see what it was. I wanted to go.

"I had experienced religion in prison before. Remember the Lucasville riot I was involved in. I had experienced the Catholic priest and the chaplain looking out of the control center port and they both had shotguns in their hands. These were men of God willing to use shotguns on other men. I asked myself, 'What kind of religion is that?' and it soured me.

"I remember at another prison, something had happened in my family and I went to the priest and he got frustrated and started cussing at me. But at that Kairos weekend, I wanted to see what had happened.

"At that weekend you (BF) were the table clergy, and I don't know if you realized it or not but I listened to every word you said. There was a time you spoke about gifts— where God picks those people to be teachers, or to be administrators, or to be laborers, or to speak in tongues and give interpretation. That confirmed my opinion that you were a 60s flower child that never really came back, because I didn't believe it. You told me when I came into the Kairos room—I always had a habit of turning my badge around so people wouldn't see my name—but when I came through that door you knew who I was, and you told me God had something to say to me that weekend.

Funny

"I remember all weekend you wanted me to go behind the curtain to pray with you and I dodged you. I thought I had dodged you successfully. Then we went into the cafeteria at the end of the weekend. I knew how the weekend would go so I knew this was the end and that I had been able to dodge you. It was then you asked me to go pray and I told you 'Yea,' but then you had a couple chairs set up back in the back of the kitchen. I had told you yes, but what I really wanted to see was what the scam was.

"We sat down facing each other and you took hold of my hands and we said the sinner's prayer. Then you let go with one hand and put it on my head and you started praying in tongues. When you put your hand behind my neck, I understood what you were saying and you were speaking things that no one knew, things I had never even told my wife about. My first reaction was to pull away because I was crying. I was mad at you because I thought somehow you found these things out and you were willing to use them to coax me into believing.

"When I left that kitchen, I had made some decisions. I knew I had to change. For my own peace of mind, I had to change. I didn't do it to get out of prison, because at that point I didn't think I would ever get out. I didn't do it for my wife, and I sure didn't do it for the warden; I didn't even speak to her. There was a line and she was on the other side and I wasn't going to cross it. I just knew something had to change.

"At the time I was running the Aryan Brotherhood gang and I couldn't do that and serve God at the same time. I've been many things in my life but a hypocrite is just not there. I could do one or the other but not both.

"*I knew how the Aryan Brotherhood was supposed to deal with me; they were supposed to kill me.* When I quit, they were supposed to kill me. I knew that, but I knew God had not spoken to me the way He had just for me to go out into the population to get slaughtered. There was something more; to this day I don't know for sure what it is, but there is something more.

"A couple days after the weekend the warden wanted to sit down and talk. She started talking and she really opened her heart to me and she started crying. That was as close as I had ever been to a prison administrator, let alone a warden. What she said to me was that there had been so many times she wanted to approach me but she knew she couldn't. And when she left the prison she would worry, not just about her staff, but about the inmates; she would worry about me—worry that she would get a phone call that I had gotten killed or killed somebody. She told me she used to pray for me and for the other inmates.

"To see that genuineness in a person and know it is just so real; that was a moment in my life that I made a decision—I was going to watch her; I wanted to be a part of whatever the Lord was doing. I bought into it and I told her in my best tough guy attitude that as long as she dealt with me as a Christian woman we would be all right, but the moment she put her warden hat on I'd have nothing to do with her. I told her that I would have to get together with all the Aryan Brotherhood members and let them know I had made a decision.

"She let that happen, and we met in the chapel. Actually what they all thought was that we were going to be transferred to a maximum-security prison. I told them something had changed and I wanted to see what God had for me. One of the brothers I was real close to started crying and he turned his back on me. None of them could believe what I was saying.

"I told them they could get together and pick a new leader and that they could deal with me however they were supposed to deal with me. I knew what the game was about; I knew what to expect.

"They got together there and talked. One of the brothers came back and told me they respected me and loved me and they were not going to pick a new leader, and I told them that we were going to be making changes and they would have to respect that and they said they would.

"I had the opportunity to watch God unfold in their lives. They started going to church and getting involved in Kairos. One by one they were giving their lives to the Lord. As a result of that—and it was God—the Aryan Brotherhood was pretty much taken out of that institution.

"They were still there physically but there was no gambling, no drugs, no extortion and nobody was allowed to put their hands on anyone. All that violence and crime was just taken out of there. We were able to reconcile ourselves with some people we had disrespected, with some other groups, some other gangs; the whole atmosphere just started to change."

BF

"How did you go about that, John? What specifically did you do to change the atmosphere or the climate?"

John

"Actually, I took the lead on that, and I started at my Kairos weekend closing. I got up to the microphone and I told all of them that I didn't know what was going on, but that something different was going on in my life now, and I apologized to people in the audience that I had offended. I apologized to the administration, and I made a vow that I would not create another victim. *(Author's note: I was present and the whole audience stood and cheered with that announcement by John.)*

"An example of that is when the warden later told me that she attributed the change in my life to have affected literally hundreds of people in that prison. That might have been a catalyst, but it was God. God had a plan for that. He just used me to do it.

"As a result of all that was going on and changing, those Aryan Brotherhood guys all went home with the exception of one, and that is because he is doing so much time. God is using him so much, that when he went to the parole board and they denied him parole, he wasn't mad about it, and he told me God needs him there for a while. I believe that; God is raising up some of those that other people pay attention to and who are strong brothers.

"When I first went to that prison (MCI), it was designed for guys like me. I was slick enough not to get caught doing the things that would send me to a maximum-security prison, but not slick enough to hide everything either. They knew what I was doing. That is where they dumped guys like me. But guys like me thrived at places like that, because we could do and get away with pretty much what we wanted.

"Then they sent the new warden there. God had a

plan for that to take place. God has ordained things throughout history and He has picked those people for it who are best suited to take that job on.

"One thing I have learned from this warden— believe me, I have studied her—is that God has empowered her and she in turn empowers people and puts them in position to do the will of God. If you look back through our history, all the big changes that have been done were not done by big groups of people; they were done by small groups that were empowered to empower others. That is what Christ did.

"God sent His Son, and He empowered Him, and He, in turn, empowered others. So 2004 years ago that all started, and look where it has taken our world today. This kind of thing shows up in the most unlikely places. It's like a cliché, if you are not sick you don't go to a doctor. The doctor goes to where the sick are at; and the prison is full of sick people. One thing the prison is good at is to bind you up to take things away from you until you get to the place that you have nothing. Then you adopt a real crazy attitude that 'If they don't care, I don't care.'

"What I have experienced in the prison is that most of the guys are just dying to be loved; that desire played a big part in me. I was starving for it; I didn't know it, and I didn't realize it. The strongest love in the world is Christian love; God's love for us. I have been so blessed to see God's love unfold—that is the payment for me. If I never got anything else, just seeing that would be enough: to see heathens just change in every aspect of their lives, not because they think it is going to get them out, or get them anything. What it does is give you that peace, that foundation, just to experience it.

"A good example is when we had that Torch weekend, the Kairos for the younger offenders. I was blessed with the job of coordinator, and by the weekend, my work was done. I got to just sit back and watch God. I got to see God. The faces would light up. You could see the faces light up saying 'Now I get it.'

"One of the things we do on that Torch weekend is we

get to know each of the young guys, and during one of the talks we gave them a cake; each of these young men would cry and break down. The majority said that was the first time they had ever had a birthday cake. We had a real problem with that part of the program because they were keeping the cakes for months. The correction officers would do a shake down and they would find these hard moldy cakes. The officers would tell them they had to get rid of them but they didn't want to.

"I always thought when God spoke, it was going to be thunder and lightning or the burning bush, but I learned that it is just not that way. It is those very little, intimate things that happen, things that you will miss if you are not watching. *People want to model what has happened at MCI but there is a piece that they miss. They pick who they think should be the taskmaster; they pick who they think should be the straw boss and run things, but they are not listening to what God has to say and what God does. They miss it, because they miss God. They can talk about the need for Him in their lives but they are really not tuned in to His presence in the little things of life; they are busy and get preoccupied with their own thing. People just plain miss God by not seeking to stay in His presence.*

"We had the guy who ran the whole prison system in Romania come all the way to MCI with an interpreter to ask us *'What is your secret?' There is no secret. It is God ordained—and you listen and do what God wants you to do. That is what is missing with most people who want to copy what has happened here at MCI.* They want to do what they want to do, what they think is best, and not what God wants of them."

BF

"Let me tell you the pattern I am seeing, and then I would like you to address that.

"The missing piece is, in part, the fact that we look outside ourselves to see things change. We will

look for processes, or programs or activities, so we can manipulate things to see something happen out there, outside ourselves. *But the missing piece is that if you are going to change a community, as MCI was changed, it has to start with change in the individual. Then that individual will help to change another individual, and that will just keep continuing. When there is a critical mass of kingdom people, it will be acceptable for others to change.*

"Somewhere along the line, it became acceptable to carry a Bible, to pray, to have Christian fellowship at MCI. That did not happen without change in one individual after another along the way.

"Now, as you respond to that, I would like you also to address the fact that the Aryan Brotherhood was a force to be reckoned with in that prison. They had power and they had influence among the prison population. Had it been some other group that did not have the power or influence, then change would have been much more difficult. Nevertheless, it seems that as you were being changed and becoming submitted to God, there came a point where your top lieutenant changed, and there then came a point where other Aryan Brothers changed. Now it was becoming safe for others to talk to the Aryan brotherhood members.

"Let me give you an example, John. A number of other men and I were outside in the prison yard at one of the Promise Keepers events and I was sitting on a bench outside with another inmate. He was telling me about the change that had taken place at MCI when your old lieutenant came to sit with us. The guy accidentally spilled his pop on your old lieutenant, who jumped up and said, 'That's OK man, accidents happen.' When he left to get something to dry the pop, the guy said, 'See, that is what I was talking about. Six months ago he would have taken my head off. You could never believe what he was like.'

"Those were the kind of changes that came from you to your lieutenant, and then to the other Aryan Brothers. That change was watched and seen by the other men in the prison. So the fact that there was a strong, influential group that was changed enhanced the speed of the transformation at MCI."

John

"Yea, I agree with you, but I don't think it was the warden's idea or my idea. God knew who He needed to touch. We were not the only group to change. At the time the Aryan Brotherhood was active at MCI, there was also the Crips, there was the Bloods and there was the Latino Kings. What God did was act in my life, and from that, some key changes took place. He didn't just act in my life; He acted in many other believers' lives also. Now my having gone through the Kairos weekend before most of the rest of the leaders may have been the catalyst. That made them watch, and then say: 'I want to do this too; I want to change; I don't like what I'm doing; I don't like who I am.' *There are hundreds of stories like mine where God just touched their lives.*

"I changed a lot of things inside my own group. I was also an active part of some other groups that were there. What it did was open people up, like what you said with my lieutenant—people could approach him. *God opened up a way for us to start crossing lines with other gangs, which was a miracle from God. Instead of our meeting on the yard to stab each other, we had something in common now*. We met on the yard for Bible study; we met on the yard to talk about prayer and share groups; we met on the yard to say, 'Look, we are all trying to make a change here and one of your brothers is way out of line and causing a lot of problems. Why don't you speak to him?' Biblically it says to approach him in private, and if that doesn't work, approach him as a group. *We intentionally started putting those Biblical principles in practice.* It started changing.

"One thing about prison, there is a lot of violence there, but people don't seek that violence out. If you are a predator in prison, one of the worst things they can do to you is lock you down 24/7 until you get out. You will do every day of your sentence and that is what they will do to you. So unless a person is on a mission to destroy himself, there are very few people who will intentionally seek out violence like that. So long as there is a different way, so long as you give someone a way out, my experience is they will always take that way out.

"Ideally, as a group, we would approach people; we would want them to do the right thing. Ideally, you would get involved in the church, but that is an individual thing, which was their choice. Whatever they decided they wanted to do about going to church was their choice. *However, coming together across gang lines like we did, as a church, rather than as an individual gang, brought us together.* We became Christians and we started dealing with things on a Christian level.

"What the coming together did was open up dialog. Before, if I was in a group with the Aryan Brothers and someone started walking toward us, that was an act of aggression and he would never make it. In order for a person to speak to me, or to one of the Aryan Brothers, they would have to send somebody and we would send somebody; they would talk and we would get a sense of what was going on. Then we would part ways and decide if we were going to talk or not.

"You know, when God started working, all those barriers, all those walls, were just taken out of the way. My lieutenant was a pretty terrible person; I liked him like that, I made him like that and I raised him like that. He was my lieutenant for years. You could see it happen in him when he made that change, when he made that commitment; everything just kind of flushed out of him. He went from that scowling face, to a sparkle in his eyes, to a smile on his face—and it was a good thing. Because what happens, guys will come into the system not necessarily doing a lot of time, but after they are initiated, after they go through whatever they need to go through to survive, they start stacking more time up. Where a guy could have gotten out in two or three years, he turns it into 15 or 20 years. I wanted my guys to go home. I wanted to give them that shot. I wanted it for them as their leader.

"If you are a leader you are supposed to want the best for that person, but with all the junk we were doing I wasn't showing love for my guys in the Aryan Brotherhood. I knew that night at the Kairos closing that I was different, but what was I to do with it? I didn't know; it would be nice if God would give us an agenda but He doesn't do that. You just pick up and go.

"The one thing I really want to touch on is the absolute necessity to be sold out and submitted to Him and not to yourself. People will say yes, yes, but do they really mean it with an absolute? God's promises are absolute. He says to us 'Bring Me your best.' What that means to me is when it is put upon me by God to do something, I do it. Whenever someone asks me to do something for Him, I do that because I am sold out to Him. Many people say they are sold out to God and that He is the most important thing in their life, but what they live out is doing their own thing or making their own decisions."

BF

"Was there any kind of planning or strategy that took place between you and the warden as to the kind of change that was to take place in the prison once the two of you started communicating?"

John

"Absolutely! What it was exactly that we wanted to see, we just didn't know for sure; we didn't know what it would look like. We didn't know what God had handed us, but we knew we had favor. So we would look at the need. What did we have a need for? And we would pray on it, and depending on what we got back, we would move on it or we would wait. We would wait for confirmation on something.

"Did we put strategy together? Absolutely! One of the things we knew really needed to happen was for people to get prepared, to get a good foundation in Christ, so they would understand what they were

really committing themselves to. By that I mean, out on the street there are many churches you can go to, take a couple classes and they will baptize you. But when you ask those people what their baptism means, they don't know.

"There are churches galore that will tell you that you need to go out and speak about your faith; that you need to evangelize. People say, 'OK, but how do you do that?' So they give you a couple classes. Does that make you prepared and ready to evangelize? No. There was a real need for that kind of foundational training. We looked and there were a lot of volunteers that were willing to do that, and there were a lot of volunteers that were active in their church that would come into the institution. But no one knew the other existed. *One of the things the warden taught me was to network, to bring people together. Take advantage of what you have, look at what they can do and empower them to do what they are good at, and just get out of their way.*

"You (BF) and I have talked many times about the different ministries you wanted to do at MCI, and your questions to me were 'How would she receive this?' I would say to you, 'Put it on paper, give it to her, and let her run with it. She is going to have to have something to show her boss.' She would say yes every time she could, but when she gets questioned about it by higher-ups, she has to have a proposal or something on paper.

"We talked about this Exodus program—President Bush calls it Excellence. He has put funding aside for it and it is for faith-based prison programs. We started putting that together six years ago, before Bush ever became President, because it was something that was put on her heart, and we knew it would come to be and we wanted to be ready for it. It is here now and we are ready for it and already getting things done, while other people are trying to step up to the plate and get things together to get a piece of it; we are already there.

"Everything that we did was all Christian-based, right out of the starting gate, and if we couldn't do it that way then we wouldn't do it at all.

"The Juvenile Offender program, which I wrote 15 years ago, just couldn't get off the ground. I tried three or four times and it just wouldn't go. I turned my life around for Christ, made some changes to the program to make it Christian-based, and let everybody know what it was from the beginning. We didn't try to hide anything, didn't mask it and that program is now in 31 states. They just completed doing a weekend retreat at the maximum-security juvenile joint right here next to MCI. They let every kid that comes to that joint go through the program if they want to, and just like the guys here at MCI have changed, that juvenile facility is changing."

BF

"Let me ask you about people who came to MCI to get and to copy programs. There is almost always a series of focus groups with the inmates for them to talk to, so inmates are aware of what they are after. The warden told me that it seemed that one of the roles of MCI was to pilot programs. Those programs are being piloted here at MCI and going out to other prisons all over the world and yet none of those prisons are being transformed like MCI. What is your opinion as to why?"

John

"That is simple; it is because the prison administrators are not Christians. They just don't have a heart for it, and they are not honoring what God wants them to do. They are doing it to fluff up their résumé, to make themselves look good. It is a selfish act. I've watched the programs fail here in Ohio. At one time the State Prison Director was sending all the wardens here to MCI to get a good piece of this. We sat down and made manuals of all the programming from ding to dong, everything that we did. The difference was they were secular people, they were not sold out to it, and they weren't willing to do what needed to be done to do it successfully.

"One of the wardens that came here is a good

example. He was not a Christian. The Aryan Broth-
erhood gang at his prison was causing him all kinds
of problems and my ex-lieutenant told him, or asked
him, "What is your relationship with God?" That
warden didn't think that was important and told him
so. My ex-lieutenant told him that God simply would
not honor anything he did until he honored God first
from the heart.

"The only thing that warden was sold out to at the
time was to make his prison different. Everything he tried
failed until he finally got down on his knees and surrendered to the Lord Jesus Christ. Ever since he has gotten
on his knees and truly surrendered, everything he has
touched has turned to gold. He is given confirmation every day that he is doing the right thing. His prison is
changing; if there is ever going to be a second MCI it is
going to be that prison.

"A piece of advice that I gave that warden was that if
he was having a problem with a gang down there he needed
to do what the warden here did. He needed to find who
the leader was, put that warden stuff aside and get an
understanding among the men; let them know he was a
Christian man, set some rules down and go from there,
instead of being that warden."

BF

"One of the things I need to deal with is a whole body
of literature on the subject of changing the climate of an
institution; all that information is secular. Some very so-
phisticated research verifies climate can and does change
in an institution. The problem is that people, who do not
have a heart for Christ, are in the business of being change
agents in institutions and schools. There are business
organizations and schools in existence today that when
someone just enters them the hair will stand up on the
back of the neck. This happens because it is a dark place
and it is not friendly and there is a negative, hostile atmosphere. In other places someone can go in and there is a
totally different climate; it is radiating with a friendly,

positive and happy atmosphere.

"How do we get that positive climate? Well, there are some schools and businesses with positive climates, or atmospheres, and they are not Christian. What is the difference between what you are saying about change taking place because of being Christians and change happening in those places where non-Christian change agents are successful? Those non-Christian change agents can go into a situation, whether it is a school or institution, and create a climate where people can enjoy going to work or going to school, and where people have peace and are friendly."

John

"Be it a Christian program or a secular program, an Aryan Brotherhood gang, a motorcycle club, an educator, or an administrator—if the leadership is sold out to the ideal of what they are doing, the example they set will be seen by like-minded people and that will cause change. Do you understand what I'm saying? I have taken so many secular programs; I have taken them all, stress management, anger management, college courses, vocational school, whatever. I've met people teaching these programs on both sides, those successful and those not successful. Those successful people believe in what they are doing, are well versed in what they are doing, and they are sold out to what they are doing. The ones not successful are those who are there to get a paycheck; they don't care one way or the other. Prison is the place to get programs if you want them. They do have some people who will train you, and they will be successful at it, because they believe in what they are doing.

"An example of that is a person I met at MCI. She does a secular program, but she is sold out to the program. The program is to open yourself and deal with your issues so you can get along with people. That is probably a real hard thing to teach because prisoners have so much baggage. But she is successful at it because she is sold out to it even though it is a secular thing. She herself is a very spirit-filled Christian.

"If at MCI they replaced the warden with someone who was not a Christian, that place would go downhill quick. The people who have been touched would still exist; but as far as the program that goes on there, the outreach at the level they have now would stop. She was the warden at another prison before coming here, but she didn't have the sold-out Christian attitude she has had at MCI. She and I have had some good conversations about that. Her Christian walk when she was at the other prison amounted to her thinking that being a good person and attending church was being a good Christian. She didn't understand the difference until she went on an Emmaus weekend and that started to open her eyes and has made a difference for her. She has been growing ever since. The Lord has picked her for the leadership role. She has been a good strong Christian for many years now, but if you asked her to quote Scripture, she can't do it. If you asked her to preach a little, she can't do it, because that is not what God has called her to do. God has put her in the place of leadership at MCI and that is definitely her calling.

"I don't care where you go in life—if you like what you do you are going to affect people. You can make a good argument that secular programming works as well as Christian programming, but I don't think it does. I personally have a whole stack of certificates from secular programs, but there was always something missing, and that missing piece was my personal relationship with Jesus Christ.

"I believe you can use your natural abilities and your own mind to be creative and do things like change some climate in a prison, a business or school, but that is much different than submitting to God and having Him open doors and provide the way. God always gives more excellence to those submitted to Him and in His will."

BF

"Just one last question, John. Is there anything you

can tell me about MCI that will help me understand how to translate what is going on there to a city?"

John

"I think that what God has done at MCI is to create a model to be carried on in other prisons and in cities. *The key people making these changes at MCI have been raised up by God and put on a path.* All the guys I worked with who are now taking seminary classes, are being prepared for when they are leaders, for when they get out and they step up to the pulpit. God has an agenda and He empowers His people and you have to get on board with His agenda or you miss it.

"God has raised up His people in MCI and they are no longer going from prison to prison, but they have been changed, and they are going back out into the community. *"You have to be broken and sold out, and you have to be willing to step through the doors that God opens, on His terms, if you expect to see God-directed change and if you expect to hear God say, 'Well done, good and faithful servant.'"*

SUMMARY

Even though John Beason committed a lot of evil before he gave his life to the Lord, he was forgiven and he became as committed and as sold out to Jesus Christ as anyone you will find. He led more people to the Lord than most of us could ever hope for and has been responsible for untold numbers of others coming to know Jesus.

John has provided us with excellent firsthand insight for how the MCI model can be transferred to our cities. He shows us what the work of transformation in America looks like.

Job 22:21 (NLT)
Stop quarreling with God! If you agree with him, you will have peace at last, and things will go well for you.

IN THEIR OWN WORDS

PERSONAL INMATE TESTIMONIES

This chapter is composed of the personal testimonies and experiences of a number of inmates at MCI who have experienced first hand the movement of God in that institution. The best way for the reader to get a feel for the transformation that is continuing to take place at MCI is to hear directly from some of those personally affected.

What follows are their own unique thoughts and words presented in their own way of talking. Again, no attempt has been made to correct their language or grammar so that the reader can get the flavor of their love for the Lord and for their zeal and fervency.

It is important to note that not all those incarcerated at MCI are like the men from whom we will hear. MCI is still a prison and there are violent criminals who need to be there for the protection of society. When these violent criminals are assigned to MCI, they find themselves in a place where many men are definitely honoring God. In many cases, the Christian environment has a positive impact on their behavior, as can be seen by the reduced violent incident rate and grievances at the prison. *Sin, evil and crime are being pushed out by the presence of the light of the Lord. That light is reflected in the peace and righteousness of a large number of inmates.*

Each day there are transfers of inmates in and out of the prison population—sometimes as many as fifty or more. Therefore, the environment changes daily with this coming and going. As a result, even though MCI is being transformed, it is not always a safe place. For that reason, I will be obscuring the identity of those quoted in this chapter for security and safety reasons.

DM

"When I was seven years old, I pulled my first burglary and when I was thirteen years old, I pulled my first armed robbery. I chose to be a criminal. That is what I wanted to do. It wasn't from my family or anyone else. I enjoyed crime; I enjoyed sin and I didn't want anything to do with God. I didn't care about God and that was just the way I lived. But sin is an awful darkness and it can sear your conscience bad. You don't even realize you are doing wrong. You will call wrong right and right wrong.

"I went through this lifestyle until I was in my thirties. I heard the gospel of Jesus Christ at least a hundred times. You see, I was dead to God; I didn't want anything to do with God. If anything spiritual came in my ear, it just went right out the other ear because I was not understanding what was being said.

"One day, God the Father opened up my ears and I heard the story of the gospel of His Son Jesus Christ. And I didn't even really know I was saved until one day—you know I used to love to drink, then one day—I looked inside for this desire to drink, and I noticed it was gone, it just wasn't there. And the desire to steal wasn't there. Then I realized there was a brand new me inside me and I didn't put him there. But then the most wonderful thing of all was that I realized I was not alone. This was within me, and all those former desires that I had, was gone. The greatest thing in my life was falling in love with Him.

"One thing Jesus Christ has done for me in my life is there will never be another victim of my crimes. I have done twenty-eight years in prison; I started doing time when I was a kid, now I'm finishing up a fifteen year sentence. I know that when I go back out there I'm not going to be committing crime. What I'm going to be doing is being a good husband, being a good father, being a good citizen, because, you see, that's where the values are in life.

"The one thing He has given me more than anything is knowledge of Him—to know Him, to think about Him, to wonder about Him. Just knowing Jesus—just loving Jesus—is the very center of my life. I would be amiss if I didn't say to whoever is receiving this (message), that if there is something going on in your life that is giving you no peace, I would suggest that you check out Jesus Christ. The Lord said, 'Taste and see if I am good,' and He is good."

FK

"I've been incarcerated 12 years now and I want to tell you about my change; but before I do, let me tell you about the one who changed me—Jesus Christ.

"I lived a life of sin and at an early age I became very bitter with God. I had gotten sick and I blamed God for my sickness, and because of that, I was propelled into a life of anger and rage and it wreaked havoc on my family members and friends and my community throughout my adolescent years. As I got older, I got involved in drugs to try to control my anger but it flipped on me and made me even angrier. I became more violent. I began pulling robberies and burning down properties and doing everything I possibly could to hurt people, because I was hurting. **Since I've been saved, what I've come to realize is: the reason why I was doing what I was doing is because I was hurting—and it is hurting people who hurt other people.**

"When I caught my case I was in the county jail, frustrated, beat down, tired from, you know, everything I had been through, and a guy came to me with the gospel, but I wasn't really trying to hear it. This guy came to me and told me, 'I've got some good news about your freedom.' That got my attention.

"Instead of telling me about the judges, the prosecution, and the whole legalistic system and how it worked, he told me about Matthew, Mark, Luke and John and how they had been with Jesus and how Jesus had set them free. He quoted a scripture of how Jesus had said, 'Come unto me all you who are burdened and laden down and I will give you rest.' That got my attention because I was so tired. The life I had lived had weighed me down so much that there wasn't nothing I could do. You know, after hitting rock bottom I came to terms that there was only one thing I could do and that was look up.

"I was in the yard not too long ago talking to a guy who told me about his recent conversion; that when he gave his life to God, he said not only did God take it and change it, but He gave it back. After getting saved, I became a new creature in Christ, you know. The anger was gone, the bitterness was gone, the resentment was gone. I felt so good that when I came into the county jail, I was five foot eleven inches, but when I left, I was six feet tall. He had straightened me out; He had made me a new man. All praise is to Jesus Christ.

"I want you to know it wasn't the time I spent in prison that did it. It wasn't the frustration of being there, because I've done time, and I've done time with guys who have done ten, fifteen and twenty years and gotten released and have come right back; it wasn't because they couldn't adjust to society after being locked up. It was because that sin nature wasn't dealt with. But with Jesus Christ, Jesus not only changes a man's mind but He changes a man's heart. The life I live today I live by faith in Jesus Christ. It is not I that live; it is Christ that lives in me."

AJ

"When I came to prison, I didn't know the Word of God. I was a real, real baby in Christ. The Holy Spirit came into me in this penitentiary, MCI, and made me look at the Word of God, live the Word of God, feed on the Word of God. He has prepared me for when I get out—I will speak the Word of God.

"The Holy Spirit is in this prison and is using men in here—preparing men—so that when they get out there, they can teach the prostitute and the drug addict and the people that are lost out there. They need salvation and that salvation is Christ Jesus.

"The Holy Spirit used a man named Paul, and he wrote fourteen books of the New Testament in prison. The Holy Spirit is using men in here. Don't look at us like we are prisoners; look at us like we are saints, because we are going out there and we are going to preach the glorious gospel of Jesus Christ."

SJ

"When I came to prison, I was seventeen. It was a quick process of growing up. There was so much darkness and it was so easy for me to become a part of that darkness. My life in here pretty much resembled my life out on the street.

"I entered into the gang life. I became an Aryan Brother and that seemed to bring the family part of my life around. You know, one of the brothers told me that in the Brotherhood, each brother would die for the other.

"In 1999 my mom came to visit me. She came twice a month for the last sixteen years; when she came, I was in a white jumpsuit for using drugs. She looked me in the eyes and said, 'When are you going to grow up?' That was a big turning point in my life. It was those words, which she didn't even realize that they had cut me; they had cut me deep.

"Six months later I went through a program called Kairos. And in that program I heard a brother talk about his father being executed and him forgiving that brother who did it; forgiving him for taking his father's life. You know, after all those years of me taking a life, I didn't realize that I had forgiveness; that God would forgive me and give me a place in His kingdom. I accepted Christ October 1, 1999 and there was no turning back from then on.

"When that brother told me in the Aryan Brotherhood that each brother would die for us, you know, Christ gave me a revelation. He told me, 'I already died for you.' You know, that struck me so deep and so hard and so profound that I've had a hunger and a thirst for His word ever since. You know, one of the Scriptures that really gets me because it shows the forgiveness that He really gave to us was 1 Timothy 1:15. It is saying that it is pleasing and acceptable that Christ came to save sinners, of which I am chief. And that is how I felt, you know. I just hope and pray that God allows me to be a vessel to be used by Him."

ST

"I came into the prison system a lost man. God definitely came and moved in my life. Some ministers came and ministered to me. When the ministers brought the gospel I already knew it, but I needed to repent, to repent of my sins.

"It was hard forgiving myself; without Jesus I couldn't have forgiven myself. I got into the Word, into Bible studies, going to chapel services. It wasn't in vain. God's Holy Spirit is in the prison just as much as He is on the outside. Walls and fences can't lock Jesus out.

"I'm just chasing Jesus, just like out there I chased the money, the women, the drugs; now I'm in prison, but I'm chasing Jesus. It is a beautiful thing in here. *You know people in here wonder why the brothers in Christ have so much love in their heart, why they smile, why they go to chapel services and fellowship and things like that; why they don't respond to problems like they used to with anger and frustration. It's because they have Jesus in their heart.* I would say to anybody hearing this message, if you don't know Jesus Christ, you had better get to know Him. He is the best thing that will ever happen to you. He is the best thing that ever happened to me."

RR

"In 1999 a friend of mine invited me to Kairos here at MCI. On the first day, I'll tell you, it was not fun; there were so many people there giving hugs and I was never used to that. Not only that, but there was the guys at the table that I never speak to them and they never speak to me.

"One of the brothers from the table and me, we started speaking, and after that we started speaking more and having more contact. It was the best thing that ever happened because we started in a share and prayer group together every Thursday, and even when other group members didn't come, me and him were always there, and that was wonderful.

"The share group taught me to live a better life. Jesus Christ came into my life there and He changed my life.

"I wanted to change my own life, but I couldn't— I tried to for 38 years, but I couldn't do it. Jesus do so much in my life; He blessed me so much, because I gave my life to Jesus. Then my family got saved, my sister, my brother, then my father all got saved. I still got one more sister and I know she will be saved too.

"I look back on the things that I have done and I look at what Jesus has now done for me and I think—if I had never accepted Jesus Christ my family would be lost like me. But now, because I am saved, they are saved, and I truly believe that if I am saved my whole house will be saved and I testify to that.

"Some brothers say 'How long you been locked up?' and I say 'Oh, a couple years.' And I start to laugh. They say 'Come on, how long?' And I say, 'Since 1981.' They say, 'That's 23 years; why do you laugh?' And I say, 'Because I'm free. My body may be in prison, but my mind is free because I have Jesus Christ in me.'"

RL

"In 1989 I came to Marion Correctional Institution as an 18-year-old man with a long time to do in prison. I was confused and scared. It was a violent, dark and ugly place.

"About three years after I got here a fellow invited me to a Bible study. I went to the Bible study with no expectations, but I was really impressed upon to have a relationship with God at that time, and the fellows began to share with me and to mentor me.

"Over the course of some years they taught me what it was to be a Christian, a man of God, and it was a difficult place to do that, especially in this institution. There were very few programs, there were very few things that were going on in the institution, and being a Christian here was not something that was accepted. There were probably about 15 brothers who were strong Christians and who were active in the church. They were the ones that picked me up and taught me what it was to be a Christian and to be a man of God.

"As time went by, something started happening here in this prison—as I said, at one point it was a dark place. About 1996 a program came here called Kairos. Kairos began to change the prison; it started bringing more people into a relationship with Jesus Christ. Since that time we have seen an explosion of programs here at the institution. Kairos led to Promise Keepers, and Promise Keepers led to different Discipleship groups and to the Horizon dorm and all these different programs.

"What has happened as a result of the programs, there is a Christian community here in the prison. *At one time, it wasn't safe to walk down the hallway, but now you see smiles, you see friendship, you see brotherly love and the Christian community has grown to where there are hundreds and hundreds of men who are actively participating in Christian events.* At the last Promise Keepers rally, there were over 400 men that attended. To see that in a correctional institution is amazing; that's over 25% of the institution. And in 1991, there were only about 15 men.

"Only God can bring about that kind of change.
Only God could bring the type of people as volunteers in
here to us, to show Christ to us and to commit to us, to
sacrifice and to show us what it is like to be the kind of
people God wants us to be. One of the Scripture that comes
to mind is Matthew 25:36 and it says, 'You were in prison
and you visited me.' We recognize this, and we see Jesus
through the volunteers, and because of that it has caused
a great explosion of God's love here at Marion Correctional
Institution."

HJ

"I'm here right now in the name of Jesus. I come in
the name of Jesus because I know that wherever I go, He
goes with me, and that is a blessing to me now, and that is
something I want to talk about for a couple minutes.

"The life that Jesus Christ saved me from—what I was
delivered from—was a life of crime, a life of corruption. It
was a life of addiction; it was a life of shame. I can remember being ashamed of my life as far back as I can
remember as a little child. That shame turned into resentment, and that resentment turned into anger, and that
anger turned into hate.

"Jesus Christ came into my life and saved me from
that. I can remember there was a time you could run me
through a ringer and you couldn't squeeze a tear out of
me. When Christ came into my life, I actually got on my
knees and asked Him to kill me. I didn't believe in suicide, but I was in a solitary confinement cell that I had
been in for over a year. I was already doing life in prison
for murder; I was continuing in my corruption, continuing
in my addictions in prison, and my sins had destroyed my
life and had destroyed so many lives around me. In that
solitary confinement cell, I got down on my knees and said,
'Lord, I don't want to live like this anymore. If this is all
I've got to look forward to just give me a heart attack or
stroke or something; just take me off the count. I don't
want to live like this anymore.'

"My sitting here today is a testament that He didn't

answer that prayer. But in a way He did, because that old man that got down on his knees that day in that cell died, and the new man that rose up is a new man that Jesus Christ is Lord over everything in his life.

"When I first came out of segregation, I was tempted to go back into my old life style and there was a struggle going on. I was torn. I was torn between the guys that I call my brothers, my friends, my crew and that life we were doing—that life of doing dope and of selling dope and gang activity and extortion and all the things that comes with the criminal life-style.

"But I wanted to serve the Lord—and I knew that I was supposed to—so He had to root out, He had to tear down, He had to bring down and destroy those things in my life. Then He started building me back up, and right now, that's what He is doing. He is building me back up and He is surrounding me, you know, by trusting in Him. God is a perfect God and He knows exactly what we need and in Philippians 4:19 the Bible says 'My God will supply all my needs according to His riches in glory in Christ Jesus my Lord.' And by trusting in the Lord, He has surrounded me with brothers, strong brothers, brothers that put the Word in me, brothers that hold me accountable. In John 8:31 it says, 'If you continue in my Word you will be My disciple and you will know the truth and the truth will make you free.'

"Well, Jesus Christ is the truth and I am free and I am surrounded by other brothers that are free; they are living, breathing, walking, talking miracles. They have been set free from addictions, from murderous spirits, and from minds that were just polluted with corruptions. They have been set free from every type of bondage you could imagine. They have been healed from sickness, both mental and physical.

"You know, I don't have to look far to see a miracle; all I have to do is look in a mirror. If that's not good enough I can look all around me and see all kinds of brothers, every single day, that are miraculous testaments that Jesus Christ is alive and that He lives;

He lives within us and He is strong at work. There is power in His blood—and every demon, every army of hell, cannot conquer one man that is cleansed by the blood of Jesus and filled with His Holy Spirit.

"I just praise God! I have so much joy in my heart. I've been in prison for 18 years, and the joy I have in my heart, the best thief in the world can't steal it from me. Because it is unstealable! You can't defeat Christ, you can't steal from Christ; He is the almighty God, He is the El-Shaddai; you can't defeat Him, and you can't even defend yourself against Him. So if you are not living for Him right now, give up, surrender to Him, and you will experience the greatest victory in your life, and it will last throughout eternity! Hallelujah, praise the name of Jesus, God bless you."

LD

"August 1998 I was saved by the blood of Jesus Christ. That was the worst time in my life. I had never experienced such a low point before; I was emotionally and spiritually dead and I felt the world closing all around me, crushing my soul.

"My sister and I were born Catholics, and my parents were born and raised Catholics. My sister and I attended a Catholic grade school and high school. We grew up in Cleveland, and our neighborhood was a life-changing experience for me. My sister was a good student all through school; she didn't drink, smoke, mess with dope, didn't stay out to all hours of the night. She got married, has four great kids and they all live a good life together.

"I, on the other hand, decided to lead a life of crime, and my neighborhood was the place where I could become known and even rich. All of my teenage years were spent following in the footsteps of the many mob figures around my neighborhood. The only time I ever called on God was when I got myself in a mess, and I'd ask God to please get me out of that trouble and I'd be good and go to church, etc. I believed God would get me out of trouble and then I'd soon forget about the promise I made to God. All through my school years, I can't remember once learning anything about my faith or any other faith for that matter.

"I came to prison with a 20-to-life sentence for murder and continued in the same things I done throughout my life until August 1998—I was busted for smoking marijuana. Something different happened to me at that time. I let so many down, I ruined the trust I had built up through the years and simply felt as though I was at the very end of my rope. I got on my knees and asked God to please come in my life and help me. I can remember feeling right when I said that, I felt warm, and a great calm overwhelmed my entire body; I really can't find the words to describe the exact feeling, only that I know without a shadow of a doubt, that feeling was Jesus Christ my Lord and Savior.

"I attended Kairos #1 and that was a great weekend but that soon went away. I tried to make prayer and share, attended the reunion, and worked weekends on other Kairos weekends. It was all good, but there was something missing. After a year I had changed my prayer and share group many times and came to realize that all the Kairos events were just a place for all the outside and inside people to come together and boost their own egos, and talk about what stuff they had done. I was discouraged at that, so I stopped going to these events.

"Back in May of 2000 the warden approached me about maybe going to the Horizon dorm. I gave her an excuse and it was done with. What I really thought was there's no way I'm going to be a part of another Kairos 'boosting my own ego' program; I was content where I was.

"After a few weeks of the warden asking about this Horizon dorm thing, I finally agreed and moved to the Horizon dorm. The first two months in that dorm were very difficult for me. I hated everything about the dorm and everyone in the dorm. I watched fakes all day long acting like Christians when the administration and/or outside people were around, and as soon as they were gone these same people acted their normal heathen selves, and

I could not stand even the sight of them. I talked with the dorm administrator many times during those two months about moving me back to where I came from. He encouraged me to hold on and give the program the chance it deserves.

"In my living cube, there were six men: one didn't believe in God; one was there for a free ticket to a cell block; one didn't care one way or the other; one was a true Christian brother, and me, a confused and angry man.

"Our living cube had decided each man would bring a scripture reading to the family table daily. That was not going good at all because it was the same person doing that. One night that person was reading the story of Noah and the flood. He got to the part where God was sorry and He destroyed the world and everything in it. I immediately stopped the reading and asked the question 'If God was sorry, then God made a mistake, and if He made a mistake then God was not perfect.' He tried his best to find scriptures that supported the one but I became frustrated and left the table. As I walked down the aisle on my way to the bathroom, I noticed one person in the dayroom; he was a Jew. I thought, there's no way I'm going to ask him anything, he might confuse matters worse. Something pulled me to go in the dayroom and without even a thought, I found myself sitting next to him and telling him what just happened in my cube. What happened next changed my life completely.

"The Jewish guy started with 'God is perfect and here's why'; he took me from the flood backward to the beginning at Adam and Eve and then forward, back to the flood. We were in that dayroom until 2:30 am. I have to tell you that night changed my life. *I truly felt the presence of Jesus enter my heart, and a hunger sprang from the deepest, most inner parts of my soul. My stomach felt like I had not eaten in weeks. My mind was overwhelmed with a desire to know Jesus, of building a close and personal relationship with a man who endured tremendous pain, was crucified so that I might have eternal life. I could not control the tears and*

emotions that night as I lay down to sleep.
"I couldn't rest for thinking about what had just happened. I can't ever think of when I prayed the way I did that night on my knees. I sincerely believe that Jesus was kneeling right next to me with His arms around me, holding me close to His chest because I could feel His presence. If I could, I would open up my chest and show you what I'm saying because words just can't tell my experience.

"From that night, September 30, 2000, to this day I have been so hungry for a relationship with Jesus Christ. No matter how many hours I work, no matter how tired I am as I walk back to my dorm at night, after work I gather my Bibles and hit the dayroom where I've had the honor of studying with three other Christian brothers every single evening. I haven't missed an evening since then and I thank God today for all the blessings He showers me with on a daily basis.

"There are only two prayers I have; I want to be a servant of the Living God and I want a relationship with Jesus Christ."

CD

"I can look back on my life and see a lot of blessings: four wonderful sons, a ton of friends, a large family and the gift of being able to sing, play and write music.

"As I look back, I also see layers of mistakes. Under those layers is me as a small child holding my Nana's hand, listening to her whistles of bird calls on our way to church. There was a divorce and I was raised in a broken home, foster homes and a lot of abuse.

"My mom tried to keep me involved in church but by then I was living with my dad and church was just a word to him. So it slipped away from me.

"I became a singer in many bands traveling all over the world singing to pay my bills. Then came marriage and children. Children—my biggest failure! Not because we didn't have a good relationship, but because I didn't show them how important God was in our lives. I pray for someone to come into their lives to teach them because they don't write back to me.

"About one year before I was incarcerated I met someone over the internet. She was so uplifting to me, and so positive and happy. I wanted to feel this way too. She started telling me about how God has influenced her life and her children's lives. She got me so hyped that then and there I decided to learn how to have that peace. I started reading the Bible and praying, but I still felt empty. I ended up in prison.

"In this prison at MCI, I have been blessed with people I've met that have helped me understand what I read in the Bible and people who have answered the questions I have had. The empty feeling was still there, but when I was around people of faith I felt at ease and comfortable.

"Then Promise Keepers came to MCI and it was wonderful. I felt so much comfort and peace with the surroundings. I cried, I laughed, I prayed, and I thanked God for everything. Then one of the men who I had been watching and who had helped me learn and who I wanted what he had in the Lord, took me outside the Promise Keepers event and introduced me to a volunteer.

"The volunteer listened to me attentively as through tears and a cracking voice I told him of my emptiness and how I longed for peace and happiness. He showed me how to give my life to Christ, and as I wept, I realized my tears were not of anguish but of happiness.

"*The volunteer explained to me that salvation isn't like fireworks or a big volcano that explodes, but it is the comfort and joy of a rebirth, a new beginning, with all my sins forgiven. I had no idea!*

"The twenty plus years of music experience in me was for a reason. I started writing gospel songs and praising God for this gift that I could share with so many. I am an infant in Christ, but my Father and so many brothers in Christ are always going to be there to teach me how to get up when I fall, and teach me how to do the same for others. I am so thankful to be a part of such a wonderful family."

YL

"When I was in the county jail in 1994, the Gideons came visiting each week and eventually I accepted Christ as my Savior. From the county jail, I was sent to MCI prison.

"I know God was with me but it seemed like I just entered hell, except there was no actual fire. The first couple of years were a big struggle for me; I read my Bible daily and went to Sunday services, but the place was still a dark and dangerous place.

"I knew God had forgiven me of all my sins, but I found it hard to forgive myself, so I was kind of falling away from Christ.

"In 1997, I was chosen to go through the first Kairos weekend and there I was finally able to forgive myself. That is when I really started to thirst for God's word, and to be a willing vessel for the Lord.

"Since that time, I have prayed daily to do His will and doors are opening more and more each day at MCI. I feel joyful that God is shining through this prison and I'm overwhelmed to see the changes God is making throughout MCI.

"I thank God daily for giving me a talent to be used in His ministry here at MCI and to guide me wherever He needs me to go. Amen."

CONCLUDING REMARKS

In these last two chapters, you have read some of the stories from inmates at MCI. There are hundreds and hundreds of similar stories, many of which are riveting.

Almost to the person, they had to hit bottom and realize there was nothing they themselves could do in their own power to bring peace and joy to their lives. When they stopped focusing on themselves and started focusing on the supremacy of Jesus Christ and asking Him to take control of their lives, and when they began to fall in love with Him, they then received that peace. You can sense the peace and the joy they have, even from those who are still babes in Christ.

> *Jesus Christ has placed in each of these men hope, joy, peace and righteousness and that is what has brought transformation to MCI. It has not been a fantastic strategy or program. It has been the recognition of the supremacy of Christ, being in His presence, falling in love with Him and then finding ways to meet needs and extend hope with whatever meager means have been available. God has honored these efforts.*

We will now look at the missing piece in transformation that we have discovered from the MCI model.

Luke 10:17-20 (NLT)
When the seventy-two disciples returned, they joyfully reported to him, "Lord, even the demons obey us when we use your name!"

[18]"Yes," he told them, "I saw Satan falling from heaven as a flash of lightning! [19]And I have given you authority over all the power of the enemy, and you can walk among snakes and scorpions and crush them. Nothing will injure you. [20]But don't rejoice just because evil spirits obey you; rejoice because your names are registered as citizens of heaven."

ONE MISSING PIECE— MANY FORMS

There are many different expressions and manifestations of the missing piece, but there is really only one missing piece. This chapter presents some of those different manifestations and expressions of that one missing piece.

The missing piece is that Christ is all and in all, and we must submit to that truth in our entire being, and in our deeds, and we must be desperately in love with Him. Simply submitting to that truth in our head is not good enough. If we do not truly understand the difference between knowing in our heart and knowing in our head, then we must fervently seek the Lord in prayer, ask for that revelation and not stop asking until it is received.

The missing piece is truly knowing we are in the presence of Christ as true believers. It is having and demonstrating the "Mind of Christ." The mind of Christ in us comes from our total submission to Christ, from our personal relationship with Him and from our desperate love for Him. When we have that, He can manifest in our attitudes, our relations, our mindsets, our body language, our tone of voice and our non-verbal communication. Having the mind of Christ is being able to think His thoughts and see through His eyes.

The missing piece is obedience and submission to the Christ that is in us. It is the mind and heart of Christ transferred to us. The Kingdom of God will come when it has come to me personally, and to you personally, then to each of our families, so that we all become vessels for Christ. This must multiply from us to our sphere of influence.

His presence is in His true believers now, not somewhere outside us, that we should have to look outside ourselves to find Him. We live close together, in what is called the city—*we are the city—and we are the community. If we desire community transformation, we, by definition, must desire transformation of ourselves.*

Transformation of ourselves can become quite threatening, because it implies we must change. By implying we must change, that in turn implies there is something wrong with us the way we are. That is a hard concept for many to accept. Let me ask the question again—why have we not seen the revival, the changed lives and the changed cities that we desire? The answer is that something has to change. Does that change need to start "outside" our self, or does it need to start within each of ourselves? The answer is obvious if we want true change; *we must change ourselves first so that our changed lives can affect our environment in different ways than we now affect it.*

THE KEY

The key is our own personal preparation to be in God's presence. How do we do that? How do we walk in His Spirit moment by moment? How do we seek Him with all our heart?

The key is not being a spiritual warrior, or having and implementing the right strategy for changing our city, or it is not changing those things outside ourselves, including other people.

Unfortunately, as humans, we tend to focus on strategies, people and events outside ourselves, rather than on the difficult issue of looking inside ourselves, at who we are and how we need to discipline ourselves to have a genuine relationship with the Lord.

There is no one specific strategy for reaching a city for Christ. However, there is a strategy and pattern for coming into the presence of the Lord, and this topic will be addressed in Part II.

Many of us unconsciously attempt to avoid His presence, no matter how much we say we desire to be there. Some of us avoid His presence because we find it unpleasant to face who we really are. For others of us, it is uncomfortable to submit to a higher being—especially when that authority is a Spirit that we cannot see, hear, smell, taste or touch. For many of us, it is unpleasant not to be able to develop our own strategy and operate in our own strength. There is any number of reasons we quietly and subtly, and even sometimes unconsciously, avoid His presence.

Human nature, left without discipline and guidance, will focus in some way or other on what gives itself glory or credit. Humans are very creative that way. We tend to focus in very subtle ways on our own selves.

Focus is important in understanding the missing piece. The efforts to transform cities have tended to focus on procedures or processes that would change the spiritual climate in the city. This has usually caused us to be involved in doing something to change what is "out there" in the city or "out there" in the church organization or "out there" in other people. However, let us look at what is happening with the MCI model.

MCI MODEL

MCI's focus has been on individual change— changing what is on the "inside" of inmates, rather than on changing something "out there." The effort has been to get more hope, peace, holiness and righteousness into individual lives. After individuals started to change, networks began to form between individuals and groups, and they began to find others desiring the same thing; this in turn began to drive out sin and evil. Informal leaders, such as the early leadership of Aryan Brotherhood, began to find and communicate with other informal leaders. They began to change individual gang member's lives and to keep individual gang members in line with this new life of peace and righteousness.

The focus of the informal leaders at MCI was on bringing peace, hope and righteousness through their individual gang members. They also focused on developing their network across gangs to open communication

The principles of the Bible were put in place to solve problems among the different gangs and the individual gang members. The popular Prison News Network (PNN) "Men of Faith" program communicated to the entire prison testimonies of hope and peace from once well-known violent offenders.

The impact was tremendous when a particularly violent inmate would give testimony on the "Men of Faith" program that he needed to start treating others the way he desired to be treated. There was also a tremendous impact when an inmate on "The Men of Faith" program would ask forgiveness from others he had violated so the Lord would forgive him.

These were the kinds of gut-level biblical principles communicated over PNN. You can be sure that the rest of the men in the population would watch that person very closely to see if he was sincere and if he would walk his talk.

There was a tremendous impact made on the population when two rival gangs, who had been having a problem with each other, sat down and talked it out, as we are directed to do in the Bible, rather than stick each other with makeshift knives. These kinds of interactions began taking place when biblical principles were applied to individuals and to everyday life in the prison.

We can see here how the focus at MCI was placed on the changed lives of individuals.

We should be focusing our whole being on sanctified hearts, right relationships and united, fervent and selfless intercession. What is happening at MCI is an action plan for walking this out; it is an example of how it is to look on Monday morning in real life.

Our focus should be on seeking Jesus Christ with all our hearts, falling desperately in love with Him and following God's prescribed pattern for entering into His presence. That is the key to the missing piece in the MCI model and to being able to come into His presence.

Am I saying that strategy and planning and work are not necessary? No, I am not saying that at all. *What I am saying is that if we are not desperately in love with Jesus Christ and if we are not in His presence, the strategies, plans and efforts will be coming from our own strength and we will fail, or at best have only human results; we can not expect to have supernatural, God results.* I point once again to the lack of fruit in America over the past fifteen plus years of efforts to reach cities for Christ. We must acknowledge that something has hindered our success, especially when there has been success in other countries.

Can we just pass off the lack of fruit over the past years' efforts as not being God's timing? No, I do not believe so, especially when God is dramatically moving to transform cities in other countries.

BEING VS. DOING

We are not called to be preparing ourselves to be leaders, implementers, disciplers, spiritual warriors, strategy developers for city-reaching or any other activity related to "doing."

We are called first to "be" in His presence and give Him glory. There is a time for doing but it will not come until we have been through boot camp and learned to be in His presence on a continuing basis, falling desperately in love with Him and recognize Him as supreme in our life.

There must be balance between being in His presence and doing His work, but being in His presence must come first, and the importance and necessity of that must be clearly understood in the heart, not just in the head.

The doing seems to be what drives Americans—it is who we are. It is no wonder there are so many nations in the world where the Lord is pouring out His Spirit but, so far, bypassing America. One of the reasons God is visiting Marion Correctional Institution is that most of the prisoners have gone as low as they can. They can go no lower so they must focus on being in His presence.

Does this mean America must hit bottom before God will pour out His Spirit here? No, it is not necessary for America to hit bottom, but it is necessary for America to wake up. The spirit of affluence definitely has a negative effect in America. We have faith, we have belief, we pray, but we still see very few miracles and healings, or see God's presence in what we do. Why? I believe it is because we expect to be able to do well and succeed, and we have so much affluence that it is difficult not to take credit ourselves.

The world teaches us to affirm our own worth, and we have a basic need to show that we are "OK." As a result, we find subtle ways to take credit for what we do; it seems to be our way of authenticating our own value and worth. Several key books on city-reaching and transformation have pointed to the need for being in the presence of the Lord before any community transformation could be effective. However, most of us have managed to sidestep that issue.

Somehow, in our American way, we have been able to give head knowledge and not heart knowledge to the importance of being in the presence of the Lord. We have been able to convince ourselves that we really are walking in God's presence. In reality, we get so busy with doing the work for Jesus, that we have little time for Him, let alone time for being in His presence.

We must learn to trust God, and we must learn the difference between just saying we trust Him and truly walking out our trust in Him. We must be willing to let ourselves go and submit totally to God in faith. God will not use us until we learn to walk in faith. We must learn how to empty ourselves of us so that God can fill us and work through us.

TRUSTING GOD

I believe the issue of truly trusting God is a major problem we all have, and a major reason we have not paid much attention to the promptings of other writers on city-reaching about the need to be in His presence.

As we began to get further along in our desire for God's Kingdom to come to our city, did we show our trust in God by coming into His presence and seeking Him and Him alone with our whole heart, because we love Him and because of who He is? ***Did we trust Him enough that we specifically and intentionally determined that He would get all the glory for changing the spiritual climate?***

We must deliberately learn to trust God, even when it goes against what we think or want. ***We must learn to let ourselves go completely, to be able to walk in His Spirit and to walk by faith. This can only happen when we learn to be in His presence.*** When we are in His presence, we learn to discern His voice from our own voices, and from the world's and Satan's voices.

Jesus wants not only to be in us but also to work through us, and this requires humility on our part. Humility is not being modest about our own strength; it is being honest about our own weakness and our own lack of ability to accomplish God's purposes.

DESIRE OF GOD

God desires for His people to be in His presence more than we can imagine. He has been calling us to abide in Him. He desires to do the doing and for us to be in Him. We have to understand there is nothing we can do for God that He cannot do for Himself.

The ministry we are to have is that of being in submission and in obedience to Him. He has created each of us for a purpose. He has given each of us life experiences and testings so that His purpose for us will be fulfilled. He has placed in us exactly what we need to be able to stand in the world obedient and submitted to Him.

We resist God's call on our life because His call on us does not always line up with what we want for ourselves—what we, the world, and even the Christian community see as rational in terms of the world's standards. *We pray to be shown His will for our life and when He shows it to us, we pray some more—because we do not recognize that He has put it right in front of us. The reason we do not recognize it is that we want something different.* We are not willing, daily, to make the hard decision to change from what we want in our life so that we may grow into what He wants for us.

God desires to manifest His glory and power to the world in these last days through us and through other obedient and submissive servants whom He has called for this hour. It is not an accident that we are alive in this season. If we are truly saved, then the Holy Spirit has already been given to us. What we need to do is ask Him to take over our life; we must surrender our life and entire being to Him. We each have to determine in our heart that we want Him to lead and guide us no matter what He has in mind. We must willingly, without condition and without reservation, submit to Him. How do we submit to a Spirit—that untouchable, unseeable being? We do it by faith, because of God's Word.

I have spent many, many years in the church, and it has been a very rare occurrence, if ever, that I have ever heard anyone say they were not submitted to the Lord.

The problem is, they do not know what that really means; they cannot know because the fruit is just not in their lives. *We know the talk, we know all the right words to say, but we do not see a need to learn what the words really mean—we think we already know.* We avoid having to give up, or having to face those little foxes, those hidden sins buried deep inside.

We must each die to our own self and be willing to become insignificant and humbled to the point we desire only God's will be done—for His glory. We must be willing to receive nothing for ourselves, and we must learn what that really means.

The problem is we find so many wonderful people who love the Lord and who are committed to working in their church or seeing their cities transformed; wonderful people who are talented, creative, organized and well postured to lead. *These wonderful people are so busy doing the work that they do not have the time to spend in His presence, learning about Him, loving Him, desperately seeking Him, humbling themselves before Him and spending fervent—really passionate, zealous, fanatical and burning—prayer time with Him. As a result, it is their own talent, ability and strength that produces the fruit we see.* Could it be that all the wonderfully busy Christian people we see around us are really avoiding having to face their own self-reliance apart from God? Why would anyone avoid allowing God to do His supernatural work through them? Usually it is because they would have to give up control and surrender themselves to another person who lives in them.

How often do we look like Christ? We say we have Christ in us and we are transformed creatures, but how often do we really see the evidence of that power and authority in our lives? In our lives, do we have the fruit of righteousness, of Christ's character and of lost souls coming to the Lord? Do we demonstrate the fruit of the Spirit in our life?

Much of this has been said before in other books on reaching cities or transforming the spiritual climate. However, it has been ignored for the most part and practitioners have moved into the "doing" part. *It is imperative that we wake up to the fact that we must come into the presence of God, be cleansed of all sin and be 100% holy, and we must do it daily. We must spend the time to be with the Lord. God will honor nothing less.* When we associate and collaborate with others who talk the talk but do not walk the walk, we soon find ourselves compromised and find God has ceased to be involved with us in our efforts.

We must understand that God finds us worthy to bring glory to Him, and we must not allow the enemy to steal this from us; he will try. To steal from us, the enemy will use busyness, other people, fear, discouragement, rejection, division, enticements from the world, desires of the flesh, lust of the eyes, pride of life and whatever other weakness we may have.

GAINING STRENGTH

It is not easy following Christ, as most know. There are tests, trials and temptations, but this is where we gain our strength. If a cocoon is cut open to help a butterfly come into this world, the butterfly will be born deformed, weak and unable to survive. The same is true with an unborn chick. It struggles to peck open the eggshell so it can be hatched, but if someone tries to help by cracking open the egg to make birth easier, the baby chick will be born deformed or weak and unlikely to live. Both the butterfly and the baby chick must go through the struggle to develop their strength to survive.

We cannot take away the struggle; it is essential for survival. We are going through boot camp in our life here on earth. We are being prepared for eternity as sons and daughters of God, who will rule and reign in the universe throughout eternity. That is our hope, and it is the promise of God.

The boot camp here on earth is to teach us the uselessness of self-sufficiency and our utter need to rely fully on Christ. We must learn that Christ is all, that He is in all and that we must be extremely in love with Him with our whole being. We need to pray for revelation as to the unfathomable implications of that statement.

God will open all doors in order for Him to minister through us; our part is to abide in Him. He will give the courage needed, and the gifts will flow through us to allow Him to minister.

When we focus all our passion and all our efforts on community transformation, we have our focus and passion in the wrong place. ***Changes that we ourselves desire to see cannot be our focus; the Changer, Jesus Christ, must be our focus.*** Worship, submission and obedience to Him are to be our focus. ***For those of us desiring to see changed lives, changed spiritual climates and changed cities, we ourselves must be people who allow ourselves to be changed daily by the inner working of the Holy Spirit.***

Within the inner chambers of our being, in our secret places, this is where the work of the Holy Spirit must take place. We must be so consumed by that Spirit that we are not our own. That means we must be willing to allow Christ to do things that we would never think of, or consider, doing in public.

What do you think Christ would do around your friends or at your workplace if you would allow Him to be released through you? Do you think your friends or co-workers would believe you were way out of character if they were to experience what might happen if you were totally submitted and obedient to Him? Hmm, that could be a scary thought. However, we must expect and be ready to yield to that.

One of the most anxious times for the inmates at Marion Correctional Institution who attended the Experiencing God class was when they realized the Holy Spirit desired to work through them, but that they had to yield and release Him to do that.

It was an anxious time for the men because they did not know what the Holy Spirit would desire to do through them and they did not know how the non-Christians in their cellblock would respond.

When most of the men in the class worked through the issue of giving up control, they would come back to class with exciting testimonies. However, giving up control and giving up their baggage was more than some of the men could deal with, so they stopped coming to the class.

WORSHIP

By worship, I do not mean music, although that is good. *True worship is not the forms—the music, the prayers, the traditional or the non-traditional observances. All these are a call to worship, but they are not true worship.*

True worship is having God on our mind constantly and declaring who God is. True worship is to know God, to try to please God and to seek God with our whole heart. *True worship is a life-style;* we must learn to live that life-style each moment of the day and this can only happen through determined practice of humility, prayer, seeking God and turning from our sins.

How many of us can truly say we go through life as true worshipers, or even that we really try to go through life that way? We are caught up in our own busyness— with a life-style of agendas, plans, schedules, priorities and strategies. Our own "self" is forever sidetracking us.

We must have fervent, united prayer for God to dwell among us, and the prayer must be aligned with the will of God. *Unfortunately, when we develop our strategies for change, we tend to look outside ourselves at what we want to see changed, and those things outside of us become our focus and we miss being with God.*

We look at the city and pray fervently that God will change our city, that He will break the strongholds that hold our city captive and that He will break bondages of lust and addictions and abuse. Think about it—how many of us pray that God will change us? Why should we, when we see the problem as being out there in a dying world, and not in ourselves? We do not see ourselves as responsible for the demonic strongholds over the city or for the bondages holding people captive.

I hate to be the bearer of bad news, but the problem is with us. We know we have given our lives to Him; we know we are not perfect and that God is sanctifying us, but our focus is not on us; it is on the situation outside ourselves. We do not stop to realize that we are the city and that the city is changed one person at a time starting with us.

We are the light that is responsible for pushing back the darkness. How can the bondages and strongholds over our cities be broken if we, as God's people, do not break them? We will never break the grip of the enemy until we break free or change ourselves first.

The leadership that the Lord will select to break those bondages and strongholds holding our cities captive will be those persons who are totally committed to Him and who demonstrate that commitment by seeking His presence in their lives moment by moment.

SECRET OF THE UNIVERSE

We need to learn from Jesus in the parable of the vine and the branches found in John 15:1-8. *From Jesus' comments, we can learn a secret of the universe on how two can become one and still remain two. The secret is unison.* The living Christ and we ourselves actually become one person and function as one person. Separation is impossible if anyone is a true believer. We function as one with Christ and yet we remain two.

As Christ is the vine and we are the branches, we abide in the vine. Christ is the life giver and we, as the branches, are the channels of that life which we receive.

Now please do not miss this because it is vitally important. As the branch, we do things. We receive sap, which flows from the vine; we produce leaf and flower and fruit. Now, here comes the problem—we like that producing, that doing.

However, the doing is secondary to the being in the

vine. Our activity of producing is secondary to our receiving, and here is where we make our mistake; this is where we fail. *This is the key to the missing piece. We enjoy the activity of producing leaf, flower, and fruit so much that we forget we are first of all receivers of the sap, which is the life of Christ. We become proud of our fruit, and that pride steals glory from Christ.*

We become so carried away with our own activity that is producing fruit, that we forget our purpose and who we are. It is not as much fun, or as prestigious to be receivers as it is to be producers of good fruit. To be a receiver is to give credit to someone else; but to be a receiver, in this case, is also to be in the presence of Christ.

If there is no receptivity, there is no fruit. If there is no receptivity of Christ's presence, there is no fruit of community transformation. When the Lord is pouring out His presence and His Spirit in other nations, we can no longer say it is just not God's timing for America. It is His timing. He is showing that through other nations, and He is showing that in America, through what He is doing at Marion Correctional Institution.

GREAT AMERICAN DREAM

In America, we have regarded life as something we must live ourselves, although we are glad to have the help and grace of God to assist us. Even though we are true believers, we rely on our own self-activity without even realizing it. *We seem to think that because we are redeemed people we need to get on with the work. The reality is that the work is not ours but the work of the vine, of Christ, that is filling us. All we have to do is be in Him and receive from Him, and the work will get done.* However, that is just not the American way.

Our American culture teaches us that we can do anything, or become anything, we want. We have that freedom in America. All we have to do is have the drive, the determination, the perseverance and the fortitude to get the training and to make things happen. Then we can be a success in anything we set our minds to do. This repre-

sents the great American dream. It is what our ances-
tors worked and sacrificed for in establishing this great
country.

We have been taught that if we have what it takes in
our character to pull ourselves up by our own bootstraps
and work hard, we will reach success and experience the
fulfillment of our dreams. That is the American dream.
What most of us were not taught was that the great American dream would become an unfulfilled nightmare without God.

*We need to understand that our basic function is
not a struggle for success, but is a struggle for a constant recognition of Another Person in us.* The transforming of our life begins to take place when we internalize that concept. It is not just a matter of allowing God to
come into our life; it is recognizing Him in us. It is that
unison concept where two are one and still two. Another
Person is functioning in us if we are true believers. *To
the extent that we allow Him to function in full control of ourselves, to that extent we have found the
missing piece.*

The question we need to answer is who is going to be
the total master of us, who is going to have the final say?
We must recognize and submit to that Another Person living His life in us and we need to allow others to see that
Christ in us, and allow that Christ in us to receive all glory
and credit.

GETTING TO THAT PLACE

In John 14:10 Jesus says to Philip, *"Don't you believe
that I am in the Father, and that the Father is in me? The
words I say to you are not just my own. Rather, it is the
Father, living in me, who is doing His work."* What Jesus
was saying was that as the Father took Him (Jesus) into
various situations and faced Him with various needs, He,
Jesus, would know this was a call to action. As He saw
the Father moving, through the lives of people and situations, Jesus took action. It was the action of faith.

When we are in the presence of God, we are not to

be inactive. Rather, we are to be alert to the Person in us and alert to what situations He puts in front of us, and we are then to exercise faith and join Him. This requires action on our part. We are not to confuse the "joining in action" with the doing. The doing usually comes from our flesh, and from something we can figure out ourselves.

In living out the American dream, we give lip service to the true Christian way of life. However, when it comes to getting things done, we fall back on what we have been taught, and that is, we need plans, strategies, diagrams, charts, goals, targets, etc., etc., etc. We pray—we may even fast—we seek the Lord, and then we go to work in our own strength and very little progress is made, except by the world's standards.

FOUR ISSUES WE MUST SETTLE

Do we believe God can commit Himself to what we have purposed in our heart to do? Are we confident that God will support what we are doing because it will bring all the glory to Him? Can God trust us to give Him glory in all things? Are we in complete unison with Him?

Before God will completely commit Himself to the work we are doing, before He will commit Himself to our efforts at transformation, we must firmly settle within ourselves all four of the following issues:

First, we must have a true revelation in our heart that the eternal purpose of God is to bring glory to Jesus Christ. This cannot be head knowledge only; we must internalize it to the place that it frightens us that we might do anything that would steal His glory.

Second, everything we do, the work, the strategy, the planning, the implementation must—and I repeat, must— be conceived by God. Anything conceived by us could then be conceived without God, and therefore, it will bring glory to us, and not Christ.

Third, the power of God must be the source that is depended upon for the continuance of any work if that work is to be effective for Christ. God's power and intervention must be the driving force. We are only to be the vessels through which He fulfills His plan; anything less than that will be of us.

Fourth, we must internalize that the only work to which God will commit Himself must be for His glory, that is, any work of transformation—the vision, the objectives, the goals, the results of all that we are involved in. Our motives must be clean. Especially when we enjoy the work, we must guard against the pride of producing the leaf or fruit; remember, it was the life of the vine flowing through us that made it possible for the fruit to grow.

Let me summarize the above four issues each of us must settle in our own heart:

First, God's purpose is to bring glory to Christ.

Second, all the work we do must come from God.

Third, for the work to continue effectively, we must depend upon the power of God as the source for keeping the work going.

Fourth, the only work to which God will commit Himself must be that which brings glory to Christ.

Those of us who have a difficult time acting on these four issues need to seriously consider whom we really intend to receive the glory for the work we do. We are servants and we must never forget our position. Our only motive can be to serve Him by serving others.

HOLINESS

If we are ever going to find that missing piece we must continually strive to be 100% holy. Ninety-eight percent will not do! We must determine before the Lord what that 2% is that we may be holding back. One big issue is control. What if we do not like what God asks us to do? Who is going to be in control? Who is going to have the final say over what we do, say or think?

Pride is another major issue. When excellent fruit grows on your branch, it is hard not to be proud of it or to display it, while letting others know, in subtle ways, it came from our branch.

Many of us hold back that 2% of holiness, not because

of some terrible sin, but to keep the final say over ourselves. We are afraid God's motives would not line up with our motives, we fear God will want us to do something we do not want to do. This is rebellion—rebellion against God, and worship of our self, which is pride. We must recall pride was the root sin for which Satan was cast out of heaven.

Pride is a part of our human nature, and we will battle it as long as Christ tarries and we remain here on earth. Whose motives are we going to follow, the Christ in us or our own? We will continually have to make this choice, so we need to be prepared for it.

Our task in being 100% and not just 98% holy is to be pure and cleansed in our inner, most hidden chambers. *Our service to the Lord is to present ourselves holy, moment by moment, as a living sacrifice, set apart, perfectly cleansed, being in His presence. No sin, hidden away in our inner chambers, will ever come into the presence of the Lord.*

We cannot be perfect in this world, but we can be cleansed from sin and be 100% holy and come into His presence.

REBUILD THE ALTARS

If we are ever going to identify the missing piece, we must learn to line our motives and our wills up with God's will. When we offer ourselves as a sacrifice to the Lord, we usually offer that 98%. That is good, but the Lord wants 100%. In the Book of Judges 6:25-27, we see that *Gideon had to do more than just make a sacrifice. Before Gideon could be used by the Lord he was directed how to tear down the altar of Baal, which belonged to his father, and there was an orderly way prescribed for tearing it down.*

Israel was so deep in sin that the people were worshiping idols. Today the institutional church worships idols, the chief of which is self. Before God would take care of the enemy, the Midianites and Amalekites, Baal had to go—first things had to be first. *Anything we sub-*

mit to, and allow to control our lives, is an idol. Many people have bowed to fear, unbelief, doubt, insecurity, past wounds, rejection, jealousy, greed, covertness, bitterness, selfish ambition, pride and a host of other strongholds. We must tear these altars down in our own lives and erect an altar to the living God just as Gideon did.

When we erect our altar to God, it is then that the fire of God will fall on us. Each of us must put first things first. We must tear down our own altar where we worship that 2% we have kept for ourselves, where we have that little corner of our self that we keep hidden.

That final part of us must be submitted to and consecrated to God. Our motives, our attitudes, our desires, our self-talk, our thoughts all must be submitted; even that small, intimate, secret part of us we try to hang on to must go. We must become like helpless little children.

It is then the Lord will send His fire to the individual and there will be renewal, revival and transformation in that person. From there, it will spread to others because God's Holy Spirit will manifest through us. Then Christ's motives, attitudes, desires, self-talk, character, mind and thoughts will all become a part of us, and all these things will be part of the "sap of life" fed from the vine to us, the branches.

When we learn this and apply it to our life, we will have found the missing piece. *The Kingdom of God will then come to our city, not because we seek community transformation, but because we seek the presence of God in our lives.* When we begin to find one another, His Kingdom will grow in our churches and our cities. This is exactly what has happened at Marion Correctional Institution.

Does all this mean we have to be perfect people before anything productive will take place in us or in our city? No, it does not mean that. Think back to the testimonies in chapters two and three. Most of the men we heard from were in prison for murder or other heinous crimes. They were far from perfect, but they turned their lives completely over to Christ and kept themselves cleansed so they walked in holiness. We can do the same.

God's Kingdom vs. Satan's Kingdom

One last point needs to be made concerning the missing piece, and that is expectation. If we expect that our whole city will be reached for Christ and the entire inhabitants will receive Jesus Christ as Lord and Savior, we have unrealistic expectations that are not backed up by scripture.

What we can expect is polarization between good and evil. There are still bad people at MCI, and even though peace and righteousness have pushed back the darkness, the darkness still exists. Darkness will continue to exist on this earth until Christ returns and sets things right; the Bible is clear on that.

People will always have to choose between good and evil as long as Christ has not returned. It is nice to think about a utopia and work toward a reached, sinless city; but until Jesus returns, we need to focus on God's kingdom coming more and more to our lives and to our cities. We need to be aware that Satan and his demons are fighting back, and often they are on the offensive.

Many of the institutional churches today teach both love and fluff; not many teach war and polarization. There needs to be balance in the teaching. The imbalance that exists today leaves us handicapped in understanding the times in which we live. We need to understand the war we are in, and we need to understand that there is more and more hostility toward Christians as the polarization increases between God's kingdom and Satan's. However, when we come into the presence of Jesus Christ, He fights the battles for us.

The battle is in the spiritual realm, and our part is to pray fervently for His kingdom to come, to be in His presence and to take action on whatever He puts in front of us.

Jesus said He did only what He saw the Father doing. What we are to be about is learning to recognize that what is in front of us is not happenstance or accident, but is what the Father is doing.

The major key then, to the transformation of our life and of our city, is to fall passionately and desperately in love with Jesus, to come into His presence and to learn to stay there as we go back out into the world as a vessel filled with the fullness of Him. How do we do that? God has provided a pattern for us to follow for coming into His presence, and we will learn about that pattern in the next chapter. As for falling in love with Him, the only way that will happen is to set as a priority the spending of much time with Him in prayer, spending time with His Word and spending time meditating on Him; His pattern is that He must be the priority of our lives. When we get the pattern right, the glory of God will fall on us and we, as vessels, will carry that into our sphere of influence.

Colossians 1:18 (NLT)
Christ is the head of the church, which is his body. He is the first of all who will rise from the dead, so he is first in everything.

Colossians 3:11 (NLT)
In this new life, it doesn't matter if you are a Jew or a Gentile, circumcised or uncircumcised, barbaric, uncivilized, slave, or free. ***Christ is all that matters, and he lives in all of us.***

PART 2
THE PATTERN

Introduction to Part 2

In this second part, we learn about the patterns that God has provided for us to come into, and to remain in, His presence.

From the tabernacle, we learn there is a very specific way that we are to approach God. We cannot leave steps out or get them out of order if we expect to be prepared for coming into His presence.

We, as Americans, are quite self-sufficient. As a result, we tend to pray for God to give us direction and when we receive it, we tend to say, in essence, "Thank You God, I'll take it from here."

Part 2 reveals the pattern God has provided for us and the pattern He expects us to follow, in spite of our independence. This part demonstrates why we have had so little success in transforming our cities. When we learn to get the pattern right, His glory will fall.

2 Chronicles 30:8 (NLT)

Do not be stubborn, as they were, but submit yourselves to the LORD. Come to his Temple which he has set apart as holy forever. Worship the LORD your God so that his fierce anger will turn away from you.

GOD'S TABERNACLE PATTERN

5

THE TABERNACLE

During the Old Testament times, the temple (originally the tabernacle in the desert) was the way to approach God. Now, in the New Testament times, Jesus Christ is the only way to come into the presence of God.

The Bible is very clear that true believers today are the temple of God; our bodies are the temple. ***The pattern that God established during the Old Testament time, through the first tabernacle, still applies today.*** We are to learn from the original pattern God established and apply it to our own temples today, and we must learn to get the pattern right for the glory of God to come into our lives.

To transform a city today we must build a sanctuary, a sacred place, within ourselves, so God will come and dwell among us. The Bible tells us to be holy as God is holy. Those are not just words; it is possible for us to be holy as God is holy. Being holy means that we are set apart for Christ and that we are to live differently, and to be different, from the world. It means we are separated from the world for God. God has set us apart from the world for Himself. Man cannot set his own self or any other person apart for God; God himself must do it. That means He is there to help us work through the imperfections of our human nature. Having a human nature, we will never be perfect in this world, but God has provided a pattern by which we can be holy.

Following that pattern on a consistent basis will be building the inner sanctuary, the sacred place for our communion with the Lord.

GOD'S PRESENCE

God's presence among us will bring about transformation in our cities. We need God's presence to move us from Satan's kingdom to God's kingdom. This will require God's people to diligently seek Him with all their hearts and follow the pattern He has required to come into His presence. We saw this happen in the lives of many of the inmates at Marion Correctional Institution.

We know from God's Word why God gave us a pattern by which we can come into His presence. The ultimate reason is that we will ultimately be living stones in the New Jerusalem, giving praise, honor, glory and worship to Almighty God and to Jesus Christ. We must learn to get over our own agendas and to get on God's agenda so He will receive glory. No sin or imperfection of any kind will ever come into the presence of God.

The Bible tells us we are to seek God with all our heart. It is then we will find Him, but the seeking with all our heart must come first.

What does seeking with all our heart mean? It means there are to be no hidden chambers of sin tucked away in some corner of our heart that we do not want to let go of, or to deal with. We must not have a hidden sin that we keep for ourselves. If we have a hidden part of our heart that we are keeping for ourselves, we cannot seek God with our whole heart because the secret sin takes up part of our heart.

Emptying the hidden chambers was a particularly difficult task for many of the inmates at Marion Correctional Institution. They had so much old baggage stuffed away in the hidden chambers. We had a number of men leave the Experiencing God class because they were simply not ready to deal with, or give up, some of the issues they had hidden. Some of those major issues were deep hurt, unforgiveness, anger and resentment.

If there is anything at all in our hidden chambers that we are aware of that is not pleasing to God, we cannot seek Him with our whole heart. We should ask God to reveal to us any unknown sin He wants us to deal with at this time. This is why God gave us the pattern to follow to come into His presence. We must learn to follow God's pattern, moment by moment, to ensure that we stay covered by the Blood of Christ, cleansed of our sins, filled with the Holy Spirit and filled with His Word.

We are all imperfect beings. God does not reveal to us all our imperfections at one time because we could not stand ourselves if He did. As a part of being made holy, of being sanctified, God reveals areas of our life we need to change and repent of.

Have you ever noticed people who seem to have constant problems in their lives? For them, the names may change, the places may change, the faces may change but the same types of situations continue to repeat in their lives. They have not learned that those types of situations in their life are caused by sin, or they have not been willing to deal with that particular issue. Therefore, those same issues will continue to repeat themselves in their life, in one form or another, until they face what is in their hidden chamber, repent, and give it to God. *When we see a repeating problem in our life, we know there is something that we must root out and deal with.*

SURRENDER

We do not like the idea of surrender. The world tells us we need to be strong and know where we are going.

The world also tells us we need to be decisive, to have a plan and to work that plan, to have passion, and to focus on goals. There is nothing wrong with these traits, but they must be coupled with God's way, which is to be passionate about, and focused on, Him.

God tells us we must surrender, submit, yield and obey. Not only that, but we are asked, by faith, to surrender and to obey a Spirit we have most likely never physically seen, heard, touched, smelled or tasted. For rational-thinking leaders who have their feet planted firmly on the ground and on whom people trust and depend, that is a tall order. That requires moving out of the physical realm and into the spiritual.

To move from being rationally objective to being subjectively intuitive is a stretch for most of us, even though we give lip service to having faith and to believing and trusting God.

That is why we have a "missing piece." Leaders begin to think about how effective they are, how depended upon they are, how visionary they are and how creatively strategic they are, or how determined they are not to fail. They gradually begin to slip into giving glory to something, or someone other than God—this is how the world operates. We somehow have to get into our heads that God will not tolerate glory going to anyone or anything except to Himself. No matter how much lip service we give to what we are doing as being "of God," our mediocre fruit does not bear that out. God is not a mediocre God.

Rationalizations such as "it just is not God's timing," does not change the likelihood that in most cases it is our own self-involvement that causes the mediocre fruit.

In America, we are just not hungry enough or desperate enough to give up our own independence to come into God's presence. It is in coming into His presence that we must come to an end of ourselves.

The Bible asks people to give themselves up, to surrender to Jesus Christ. When we truly get to the point of realizing we must be in submission or else be in rebellion, we often begin to have some of the following conversations with ourselves: "What will happen to me?" "What if God asks me to give up something of which I do not want to let go?" "What if God asks me to do something I just can not do?" "There are a lot of things in my past that I have been able to put behind me and I am doing just fine; what if God would expect me to dig those things up and deal with them?" "I just do not want to let go of myself." "If the truth were known, I really do not think I trust God enough to completely let myself go. I have made many commitments and many people depend on me, and if God should change things from the direction I have been leading, I will look foolish in the eyes of all those godly people and my fleshy nature will be exposed."

RATIONALIZATION

Then the rationalization begins and we find every reasonable, logical reason why we can submit to the Lord and still hold back some of those secret strongholds in the deep, hidden chambers of our heart.

Some of those hidden bondages or strongholds we would never admit to or deal with—bondages or strongholds like hidden pride, secret envy or jealousy, being stubborn, having a critical nature and having selfish ambition. Some of those hidden things might be needs, such as seeking or wanting recognition, prestige, status, fame, wealth and power. It may be an inner need to say or do those things that show others we are worthwhile, like telling little white lies, or purposely, and sometimes habitually, stretching and exaggerating the truth.

Some other matters possibly buried in the hidden chambers of our hearts could be exploitation of others, in little ways that take advantage of them, and show us in a good light. It could be the need to own and control what we are doing. It could be strongly declaring the value of responsibility, yet being only selectively responsible in our own lives. It could be a willingness to overly compromise to seek peace with others. It could be our tendency to fracture relationships when things do not go our way. It could be our going into denial, even to ourselves, over our having anything at all in our hidden chambers.

In our hidden chambers, there can be no competitive spirit that desires to show that we are the best or that we are somebody worthwhile. There can be no faultfinding of others or hidden desire of being better than others. There can be no deceit. There can be no secret sin of self-gratification. There can be no secret desires for power, prestige, fame, status or wealth. There can be no sexual sins, pornography, or entertaining of lustful thoughts.

Our rationalization is ingenious and can take many forms, but many of those bondages or strongholds listed are in the hidden chambers of the hearts of most of us in one form or another. This is a major reason why we resist total, sold-out submission and obedience to Christ. Many of us are unwilling or unable to deal with what is in our hidden chambers.

God has provided a way for us to deal with the hindrances we have, whatever they are. They are to be dealt with as we follow His pattern for coming into His presence. The rewards are tremendous for those who will truly seek to find Him with their whole heart and not with just 98% of their heart.

In the Experiencing God class at Marion Correctional Institution, learning and applying the tabernacle pattern was a most freeing experience for the inmates. Coming into God's presence and learning to walk in His Spirit during the day helped the men to break free of their bondages and strongholds, and helped them fall even more in love with Jesus.

GOD'S PATTERN

God provided Moses with specific details for building the tabernacle in the wilderness. *God told Moses to build the tabernacle so He could come and dwell among His people. God is the same yesterday, today and in the future, and He still desires to dwell among His people.* Understanding and applying the pattern of the tabernacle is essential for bringing the glory of God and His kingdom to our lives, our churches and our city.

Every true believer in Christ today is God's temple. This means we must make certain that we understand, and that we honor, the timeless principles of the tabernacle that were put in place by God Himself so we can come into His presence.

Tabernacle Diagram. Following is a simple diagram of the layout of the tabernacle.

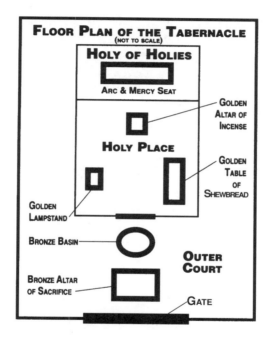

Notice the gate at the bottom of the picture; that allows us to come into His courts of praise from the world. Both the bronze altar and the bronze washbasin are in the courtyard. In the Holy Place are the lampstand, the table of shewbread and the altar of incense. In the Most Holy Place are the arc of the covenant and the mercy seat. *The Most Holy Place is where the presence of God dwelled, and where He dwells today in true believers.*

The tabernacle is a representation of the Trinity. The gate and outer court represent the workings of the Holy

Spirit in our flesh. The Holy Place represents the work of the Son, Jesus Christ, as the light of the world, as the provider of our needs and as the intercessor for the saints who pray. The Holy of Holies represents a supernatural place. God dwells on the mercy seat and we meet Him there beneath the wings of the cherubim. The mercy seat covers the arc of the covenant, which holds three supernatural items. Those items are Aaron's rod that budded supernaturally, a golden pot of manna that God supernaturally provided as food for the Israelites while they were in the desert, and the Tablets of Law that God supernaturally provided.

When we truly come into God's presence beneath the wings of the Cherubim, we can and should expect the supernatural to happen. We saw the supernatural happen at Marion Correctional Institution during the Experiencing God class.

The Walls of the Tabernacle, as described in the Book of Exodus, were 150 feet long, 75 feet wide and 7 feet high, and made out of fine white linen. There were 60 pillars on each side and 20 pillars across each end that supported the walls.

The white walls symbolized the righteousness and holiness of God and symbolized that He is set apart from the world.

When a person comes in from the world to approach God, he must do so in awe, reverence, adoration and worship. He must thank God for the privilege of entering into His presence.

We see how Jesus Christ fulfilled the symbolism of the walls from Ephesians 4:24: *"And that you put on the new man which was created according to God, in true righteousness and holiness."* And from Second Corinthians 5:21: *"For He made Him who knew no sin to be sin for us, that we might become the righteousness of God in Him."*

The Gate into the Tabernacle was 30 feet wide, 7 feet tall, and was made out of fine twined linen that was blue, purple and scarlet.

The gate teaches us that there is only one way to

enter into the presence of God, and that we have to make the approach to God ourselves.

Jesus Christ fulfills the symbolism of the gate by being the only way through which one may enter into God's presence. We see this in the Scriptures of John 10:9: *"I am the door. If anyone enters by Me, he will be saved, and will go in and out and find pasture."* And John 14:6: *"Jesus said to him, 'I am the way, the truth, and the life. No one comes to the Father except through Me.'"*

Many people today hold the popular belief that there are many different ways to come to God. They are in error. There is only one way to come to God, and that is through Jesus Christ who represents the only gate into His presence.

The Brazen Altar in the courtyard is the first item we come to once having entered through Christ, who is the gate. It is 7-1/2 feet square and 4-1/2 feet high and is made of acacia wood covered with brass. There are four horns, one on each corner, used for tying down the animal sacrifice.

The brazen altar teaches us that a sacrifice is required to be paid, by a substitute for ourselves, for the forgiveness of our sins. It teaches that there is no forgiveness for our sins without the shedding of blood, and that there is no way to approach God, no way for man to be saved, without the shedding of blood by the sacrifice of a perfect substitute for us.

Jesus Christ fulfilled the symbolism of the sacrifice on the brazen altar, through His death on the cross, as a perfect substitute for the death penalty we were to pay for our own sins.

The Laver, or Bronze Basin, is the next item we come to in the courtyard, and it is made of brass. Its size is not given. It was used by the priests to cleanse themselves after being covered by the blood of the sacrifice on the brazen altar.

The cleansing was necessary before the priest could enter into the Holy Place, serve God and carry out His ministry.

The laver teaches us that we cannot enter into God's presence without being cleansed and made pure. In addition, we cannot serve God until we are cleansed. It teaches us that we must be continually cleansed and made pure if we are continually to serve God.

We can see how Jesus Christ fulfilled the symbolism of the laver in John 13:8: *"Peter said to Him, 'You shall never wash my feet!' Jesus answered him, 'If I do not wash you, you have no part with Me'"*; as well as in, 1 John 1:7 *"But if we walk in the light as He is in the light, we have fellowship with one another, and the blood of Jesus Christ His Son cleanses us from all sin."*

The Outer Veil of the Holy Place was made of fine linen colored blue, purple and scarlet. Five pillars of acacia wood covered by gold supported the veil and was the only entrance into the Holy Place.

What the outer veil teaches us is that a person cannot just rush into God's presence. To do so shows a lack of understanding in the heart and mind of who God is in all His awesomeness. Who God is demands that we show respect. God created the earth, moon, our sun, and all the planets in our solar system. Our solar system is just a speck in our galaxy the Milky Way, and there are millions and millions of galaxies, many of which are larger than our Milky Way. God surrounds that entire universe and holds it in His hand. Yet man is the centerpiece of all God's creation. We must be in awe, with fear and trembling at the greatness of our God and we cannot just rush into His presence showing disrespect.

There is more to knowing and experiencing God than just sacrifice and forgiveness of sins. That was done at the brazen altar and the laver; there is much more than this. Many people never get past the sacrifice of Christ and the forgiveness of their sins, referred to in Hebrews 6:1 as the "doctrine of Christ." They never learn that there are much deeper understandings of God waiting for those who seek Him with all their hearts. *There is a getting past just living on milk; there is real meat for growth. There is worship in the Holy*

Place and in the Holy of Holies.

Jesus Christ fulfilled the symbolism of the veil to the Holy Place as being the only way into the deeper things of God found in the Holy Place and the Holy of Holies. The only way in is through Jesus Christ and through Him alone.

The Table of Shewbread was a small table 3 feet long, 1-1/2 feet wide and 2 feet 3 inches high made out of acacia wood covered with gold. The purpose of the table was to hold the twelve loaves of bread, which were sprinkled with frankincense. The loaves were replaced each Sabbath and the frankincense was burned as an offering to God. The priests were permitted to eat the old bread if they desired.

The Table of Shewbread teaches that Jesus Christ, and the worship of Him, is the bread of life, and the Word is the nourishment that man needs. It also taught that man must have the nourishment of His Word.

The frankincense taught that God is pleased with the aroma of man worshiping Him.

Jesus Christ fulfills the symbolism of the Table of Shewbread in that He is the Bread of Life, the nourishment that man must feed on to know and worship God. Scripture shows the Table of Shewbread as symbolically representing Christ.

John 6:33—*For the bread of God is He who comes down from heaven and gives life to the world.*

John 6:35—*And Jesus said to them, "I am the bread of life. He who comes to Me shall never hunger, and he who believes in Me shall never thirst."*

John 6:48—*I am the bread of life.*

The Golden Lampstand, or candlestick, was made out of pure gold and is the second item we come to when we enter into the Holy Place. It had a central candlestick with three other candlesticks on each side making seven candlesticks in all. It burned pure olive oil and was never allowed to go out. There were no windows in the Holy Place and the candlestick provided the only light.

The lampstand teaches us that we need light and

illumination if we are to know God and serve Him.
The oil represents the Holy Spirit, the Spirit of Wisdom
and Understanding, the Spirit of Counsel and Might and
the Spirit of Knowledge and Fear of the Lord. We could
never know or serve God without this light of the Holy
Spirit.

Jesus Christ fulfills the symbolism of the lampstand
in that Christ and Christ alone provides the light and illumination to know and serve God. This may be seen in
the following scriptures:

John 8:12—*Then Jesus spoke to them again, saying, "I
am the light of the world. He who follows Me shall not
walk in darkness, but have the light of life."*

John 1:4—*In Him was life, and the life was the light of
men.*

2 Cor. 4:6—*For it is the God who commanded light to
shine out of darkness, who has shone in our hearts to give
the light of the knowledge of the glory of God in the face of
Jesus Christ.*

The Altar of Incense was 1 foot square and 3 feet
high. The altar construction was of acacia wood and over-
laid with gold, and its purpose was to burn incense to God.
The fire burning the incense was never to go out and was
an offering to God, sending Him a continual sweet aroma.

*The altar of incense teaches that the incense was
a symbol of the prayers of the people and that prayer
and intercession were essential for worshiping God
and were to be continually offered up to Him in unbroken communion.* It also taught that the priest and
the minister must constantly intercede for God's people.

Jesus Christ fulfills the symbolism of the altar of incense in that He always prayed and in that He always
lived and walked in unbroken communion with God. Walking in unbroken communion with the Father was how He
only did what He saw the Father doing. Christ also inter-
cedes for God's people.

The Inner Veil separated the Holy Place from the
Most Holy Place in the tabernacle. It was the symbol of
where the presence of God dwelled. The construction was

of fine linen colored blue, purple and scarlet. Four pillars, constructed out of acacia wood and covered with gold, supported it.

Only the chief priest was permitted on the other side of the inner veil in the Holy of Holies, and then only once a year on the Day of Atonement.

The inner veil teaches that fellowship and communion with God is the supreme act of worship. God is totally set apart from the uncleanness of the world, and man must approach Him carefully and in awe and reverence.

Jesus Christ fulfilled the symbolism of the inner veil in that He is the only way into the presence of God. There is no other way.

When Jesus died on the cross this inner veil was torn from top to bottom symbolizing that man no longer needed the intermediation of the priest to approach God on man's behalf. Because of the substitutionary sacrifice of Christ for our sins, we are now able to approach God ourselves through Jesus Christ by following the prescribed pattern laid out by God in the tabernacle. When we get the pattern right, and seek Him with all our hearts, we are able to know, to experience, to fellowship and to commune with God through Jesus Christ.

Have you ever wondered why having a truly intimate relationship with Christ is so difficult? It is because we do not always get the pattern right or we seek Him with only 98% of our heart and not with our whole heart, all 100% of it. We hold something back in our hidden chambers, usually because of <u>doubt</u>, lack of full <u>trust</u>, or because of some <u>fear</u>.

<u>**The Arc of the Covenant**</u> was 3 feet nine inches long, 2 feet 3 inches wide and 2 feet 3 inches high and made of acacia wood completely covered inside and out with gold.

The lid, or top, of the arc was called the mercy seat and was a solid slab of gold. Arising at both ends of the mercy seat and formed from the same piece of gold as the lid, were two angels called cherubim.

The presence of God was to rest on the mercy seat beneath the wings of the two cherubim. *"And there I will meet with you, and I will speak with you from above the mercy seat, from between the two cherubim which are on the ark of the Testimony, about everything which I will give you in commandment to the children of Israel."* (Exodus 25:22)

As mentioned before, the arc contained three supernatural items: (a) the law, or Ten Commandments, supernaturally supplied by God, (b) the golden pot of manna, which God supernaturally supplied as food to the Israelites in the desert, and (c) the rod of Aaron that supernaturally budded.

It was on the mercy seat that the priest sprinkled the blood of the atonement, symbolizing that God could be approached only through the blood of a sacrifice. Jesus Christ's shed blood was sacrificed one time, and for all of us, and there is no more need of any other blood sacrifice for our sins.

The arc of the covenant teaches us that God can be approached only through the substitutionary sacrifice of a pure life, and Jesus Christ made that pure and perfect sacrifice. It is only because of that perfect sacrifice for us that we can be acceptable to God.

Jesus Christ fulfilled the symbolism of the arc of the covenant and the mercy seat by being the substitutionary sacrifice for our sins. He was the pure, sinless Lamb of God who paid the price for our sins with His own life.

SUMMARY OF THE PATTERN

The pattern of the tabernacle is so important for us to understand, I will summarize it.

Many of the men at Marion Correctional Institution knew intuitively they needed to seek God with their whole being, and they tried to do that. However, much of their baggage remained because they did not know how to deal with it, and they did not understand the pattern God had provided for them to come into His presence.

Many of the men at MCI had salvation and cleansing at the bronze altar and bronze laver and they

thought that was enough. In reality, it was just the beginning. They needed to come into the Holy Place and be filled with His Spirit of wisdom and understanding, His Spirit of counsel and might and His Spirit of knowledge and fear of the Lord. They needed to be filled with His Word, and they needed to learn to offer the sweet aroma of fervent prayer. They needed to do these things prescribed by God before they could come into His presence and commune with Him beneath the wings of the Cherubim. Learning what God required was a freeing experience for many of them, but they had to move beyond salvation and cleansing; they had to move to His presence.

The pattern provided by God, which we must all follow if we are to come into His presence, shows that we are to come in from the world through **the gate** of Christ, into **His courtyard** with praise and thanksgiving to God for providing a way for us to return to Him and His presence.

The first thing in the courtyard we come to is the **bronze altar** which represents Christ being sacrificed on the cross as a substitute for us. He was the perfect sacrifice required by God for our forgiveness. It is here that we die to ourselves, become living sacrifices, repent of our sins and ask forgiveness.

The bronze laver is the next item we come to in the courtyard, and it is here we receive the cleansing from all our sins by the covering of the blood of the perfect sacrifice, Jesus Christ.

This is where most people stop. They never get past the immaturity of the milk and move on to the meat of spiritual maturity in learning the deep things of God. They never get past the confessing of sin, repenting and asking forgiveness and covering of the blood of Jesus. This is all good and necessary, but there is so much more.

It is from here, from our cleansing, that we begin to enter into preparation for ministry and for learning spiritual truth in the Holy Place.

To enter the Holy Place we must pass through the **outer veil.** Needing to pass through this veil reminds us that we cannot just rush into the presence of God. We must show respect for who He is and prepare ourselves.

Upon entering into the **Holy Place,** we come to the **Table of Shewbread,** which represents God's Word and provision. Jesus Christ is the Word and He is our provision. We are to be filled with His Word and we are to be cared for by His provisions.

Next in the Holy Place, Jesus Christ, as the light of the world, confronts us. The oil burning in **the lamp** fills us with the Holy Spirit, and we receive the light of the Spirit of wisdom and understanding, of the Spirit of counsel and might and of the Spirit of knowledge and fear of the Lord. We are to be the light of Jesus Christ in the world through the power of the Holy Spirit.

The **altar of incense** is the next item we come to and this represents the prayers of the saints rising continually as a sweet aroma to God. Here we are to intercede for others and to pray for God's kingdom to come here on earth as it is in heaven. Here we bind and loose with the authority given by Jesus Christ. Here we have fervent prayer.

Since the **inner veil has been removed** by the sacrificial death of Christ, we are now able to approach the **arc of the covenant** and the **mercy seat** of God through Jesus Christ any time, rather than once a year through a human priest.

Having followed the pattern with all, that is 100%, of our heart and having diligently sought Him, we are ready to fellowship and commune with God beneath the wings of the cherubim. This is a supernatural place and a reverent, holy and cherished place. This is where we come when we come through Jesus Christ as holy, cleansed and submitted vessels. *Here is where we have intimacy with the Father and commune with Him in spirit. Here we receive His supernatural power and authority to return to the world.* As vessels, we carry Christ from here to the world as His ambassadors.

When we speak of the missing piece in city-reaching, we are talking about how rare it is for busy people to learn how to come into this intimate place moment by moment, as Jesus Christ did. *How rare it is to be in constant communion and fellowship with Our Father.* We can rationalize all we want that this is just unrealistic in today's busy world; nevertheless, it is what the Father wants of us.

We must make this our priority, our mission, our goal, our passion and our whole being for existence. When we do, the rest will take care of itself, no matter what God has called us to do. *The doing must remain secondary to being in His presence, and we must not continue to get the two mixed up.*

At the **mercy seat** is where God will reveal to us the direction we should go. It is here that we learn to say as James said, *"If it is the Lord's will, we will live and do this or that."* (James 4:15)

It is at the **mercy seat** that we learn truly to recognize there are many ways He speaks to us. It is here we learn to trust God and to learn to have a deeper understanding of Him.

It is from the **mercy seat** we are able to go back out into the world knowing He fills us, and we become more alert to where He is working and to what He is doing, so we may join Him in faith.

At the beginning of this chapter, we said that to transform a city we must build a sanctuary, a sacred place, so God will come and dwell among us. That sanctuary, that sacred place, is within ourself. It is first to be built within us, and then it will exist in our city through us. When He truly dwells in His people, His presence will begin to fill our cities. *We will never bring the presence of God to our church or to our city if we first do not have the presence of God manifesting through us—not just dwelling in us, which happens back at the time of salvation.*

I sense the need for a note of caution here for city-reachers. I can almost hear the wheels turning. What I hear is "OK, how do we operationalize this concept? What will this concept look like on Monday morning?"

The caution is that there must first be a true seeking to be in His presence and to be 100% holy! The doing part will take care of itself when He instructs us from the mercy seat and sends us back out into the world filled with the power and authority of His Holy Spirit. If you, or your group, determine yourselves what is to be done, then it will be you or your group who will receive the credit and glory. We know God will not share that with anyone, no matter how noble their intentions.

Being in His presence at the mercy seat does not mean once a month or every two weeks or so. It means learning to live there so often that we can commune with the Father anytime, moment-by-moment. We will never learn to be able to do only what we see the Father doing without that constant communion with Him. ***Building the sanctuary, the sacred place, requires that we make the time and set as a priority—consistently, and with determination and perseverance—following the pattern God has provided us in the tabernacle; we must learn to come all the way to the mercy seat to commune with God on a moment-by-moment basis.*** It is then we will have built the sanctuary, the sacred place within ourselves—in God's holy temple.

I believe we, who have desired to transform our cities, have gotten the process backwards; we have gotten the cart before the horse. The horse represents being in the presence of God and the cart represents doing the work.

Both the horse and the cart are vitally important; however, we must keep them in the proper order. We must be in His presence first to receive the power and authority to be able to see and hear what He is doing so we may step out in faith to join Him and allow Him to manifest through us.

GOD'S
PATTERN
IN EPHESIANS

PATTERNS OF EPHESIANS

Once we have been in the presence of the Lord we will desire to stay there. However, the Lord will send us back out into the world to be His vessels through which He may manifest. We need to know how He desires us to live, what kind of life-style of righteousness He desires us to follow. We also need to know how to walk in faith and just what that means.

This chapter will cover the life-style we need to follow and the next chapter will cover our walking in faith.

FUNDAMENTALS

When a young man joins the military to go to war, he is often impatient to get through boot camp and get on with the action. Sometimes he has a difficult time even seeing the need for going to boot camp. However, boot camp is required to learn fundamentals—fundamentals on the type of equipment used and how to operate that equipment, fundamentals of authority as well as obedience to that authority and fundamentals of living in close relationship with others. The young man is impatient to fight and eager to get out of boot camp.

The same is very often true of us when we turn to the book of Ephesians. We are anxious to get to Ephesians 6:10 and beyond, where the armor of God for the war is discussed. Verse 10 starts with the word "Finally" which means that what follows is a continuation of what went before. Therefore, when we start with chapter 6 verse 10, we are starting at the end of the book of directions and not at the beginning. This disrupts the flow of God's pattern that He is trying to teach us.

It needs to be said at this point that we will be talking about the kind of life-style needed by the believer that is found in the Book of Ephesians. However, the Sermon on the Mount in chapters five, six and seven of the Book of Matthew is also an excellent resource of life-style behavior that was given by Jesus Himself, but we will not be covering that section of Scripture in this book.

The concept of living a life-style of peace as a way to war in the spirit is a concept that must be continually emphasized with the inmates at Marion Correctional Institution. *The natural inclination of humans, and this includes those Christian inmates at MCI, is to arouse or stir the emotions to war in the natural; it must continually be kept before people to war through a life-style of righteousness.*

Let us look at the beginning chapters of Ephesians and explore the pattern that God gave to prepare us for war.

The first three chapters in Ephesians unveil the mystery of the church with the revealing of God's hidden intention. *The mystery revealed is that God was forming a Body to express Christ's fullness here on earth, and He was doing this by uniting one people with whom he would dwell. In addition, God's revealed secret intention was to equip, empower and mature this united people so that they might continue Christ's victory over evil here on earth.*

Ephesians unfolds the process by which God is bringing the church into its destined purpose in Christ, which is to be His New Jerusalem. There are basic, maturing steps that are to be taken to prepare the church for its appointed battle with the dark powers before we become that New Jerusalem.

Before the church is called to war in the last chapter, she is taught where she stands, and that is knowing what her position and authority are in Christ. Then she is taught how to walk in the world as a true believer; taught what her conduct is to be.

POSITION IN CHRIST

As the church, our position is in Christ—we see this in chapters 1 through 3. *We must understand what it means to be positioned in Christ. This does not mean we are physically located in Christ, in the heavenlies. Rather, it means we "hold the position" of being in Christ.*

If we were the CEO of a corporation, we would still be the CEO when we were at home, as well as when we were at the office. We could even be flying, or traveling by some other means, but we would still be the CEO because being a CEO is a position.

The President of the United States holds the position of president no matter if he is in his office in Washington, at Camp David, flying in Air Force One or visiting in another country. His position is that of President of the United States no matter where he is.

Therefore, we do not have to be on site to hold a position. The position we hold is "in Christ"; that means we are one with Christ. Being one with Christ has tremendous significance for us to internalize. That is the position we hold.

What do the words "in Christ" mean? What does it mean for a person to be *in* Christ? *It means that a person's faith in Christ gives him the position of being in Christ. Positionally, the person is placed in all that Christ is.* Christ lived, died and arose, so to be *in* Christ means that a person lives, dies and arises *in* Christ. Christ is the person's

Representative, his Agent, his Substitute, his Mediator in life and death and resurrection. The person who believes *in* Jesus Christ is *identified* with Christ: counted and considered to be "in" Christ; reckoned, or thought of and credited as, "in" Christ, by God.

Boot Camp

As the church, the Body of Christ, we are taught to walk in righteousness; we are taught how to live. This is covered in chapters 4 through 6:9. In the Book of Ephesians these chapters, which deal with our walk in life, uncover the "missing piece."

Many of the inmates at Marion Correctional Institution are learning to walk out their life in righteousness and that walk is a testimony to others.

For believers to receive authority, they must practice the disciplines of unity, purity, forgiveness and walking in fullness of the Holy Spirit. That is God's pattern and His order.

To be prepared to put on the armor of God and go to war, there are many things we must first learn at boot camp.

We learn that we must practice the discipline of walking in unity. For there to be unity, relationships at every point must be in order.

We learn that we should no longer walk as the unbelievers walk, that is, in our minds. We are to practice the discipline of putting off our old man and are to practice the discipline of being renewed in the spirit of our mind, putting on our new man of righteousness and holiness.

We learn that we are not to grieve the Spirit. We are not to sin if we are angry, and we are not to let the sun go down on our anger. We are to practice the discipline of not giving place to the devil in our lives. We are to practice the discipline of letting all wrath, anger, clamor and evil speaking be put away from us. We are to practice the discipline of being kind to one another, tenderhearted, forgiving one another, just as God in Christ has forgiven us.

We learn that we are to walk in love and be imitators of God. We are to practice the discipline of putting away from us such things as fornication, uncleanness, filthiness, foolish talk, and coarse jesting.

We learn that we are to walk as children of the light. We are to practice the discipline of learning what is acceptable to the Lord.

We learn that we are to practice the discipline of walking in wisdom, making use of the time we have and understanding what the will of the Lord is.

We learn that wives are to practice the discipline of submitting to their husbands, as to the Lord, and we learn that husbands are to love their wives just as Christ also loved the church and gave Himself for her.

We learn that children are to practice the discipline of obeying their parents in the Lord.

We learn that employees are to practice the discipline of obeying their employers, and that employers are to practice the discipline of doing the will of God toward employees.

COMPETENCE

When we have spent the time in boot camp and developed competence in these disciplines, we will have the skills to go out into the world after having been in God's presence, and we will have found the "missing piece" to govern our behavior. *We will be ready to live a righteous life through the character of Christ in our warfare for men's souls because we will have been in the presence of Christ.*

If all the training required in boot camp seems too restrictive, too tedious or too time consuming for you, then you are most likely not ready for God's army and the spiritual war. What you need to do in that case is to give yourself in total submission to the supremacy of Christ, spend more time in His presence and fall in love with Him all over again. *We must not go to war unprepared.*

BEFORE GOING TO WAR

If we desire to change our city so that it reflects the Kingdom of God, we must follow God's pattern and His training plan, even when that pattern requires disciplined training and learning many different behaviors in our own life-style.

God has given us the discipline of peace so that we can enter into the spiritual war. *God will give the city to the church that walks in peace. When the city gets loved in peace, the devil will falter and fall.* We must have spiritual authority in our lives first—authority that has been gained from the disciplines of peace in our own life-style as well as disciplines that have been laid out for us by God. It is by following God's pattern of disciplined peace that we are able to develop virtuousness, holiness and righteousness in our lives.

Before declaring war on the devil, we must be at peace in our relationships—that is not only between husband and wife, but also with children and other relatives, neighbors, employees and employers, and other people groups.

A major reason for the "missing piece" is that we have not understood the war. The offensive and defensive functions of the armor in Ephesians 6 are well taught to most of us, but many have been taught that the battle is similar to a human battle.

In human terms, we have the belt, breastplate, sandals, shield, helmet and sword. When these items get connected with the emotions and human soul, we are ready for war in human terms. However, these are not really the weapons; they are only descriptions of the weapons in human terms. The real weapons are spiritual and they are truth, righteousness, the gospel of peace, faith, salvation, and the Word of God.

The use of spiritual weapons rather than human weapons has been, and continues to be, a difficult lesson to learn by the men at Marion Correctional Institution as well as for us. We are not accustomed to operating in the spiritual realm.

When we focus on truth, righteousness, the gospel of peace, faith, salvation and the Word of God, we are in a different frame of mind than when we focus on the offensive and defensive weapons of warfare in the carnal, emotional, human realm.

Many of us have not understood that God has trained us to war through peace. This is not in our human experience and that is the reason we must be taught truth in boot camp. It is far different warring in peace, righteousness, holiness and worship, all in the spirit, than it is to stir our emotions and determine in our own wills that we are going to run the devil out-of-town, or out of our neighborhood.

Since no city in America has been taken back from the devil, we need to intensify our efforts in locating the "missing piece" in our lives and accept the fact that we must start doing our warfare in different ways. We must come into the presence of God through the pattern of the tabernacle and learn to walk by the lifestyle pattern He has taught in Ephesians. We need to learn that walk so well that we know immediately when we are out of line. That way we can immediately get back to the bronze altar and bronze laver for forgiveness and cleansing, and be covered by the blood of Jesus.

As humans, most of us have preferred to rely on our own intellect, our own will, our own experience, our own emotion and our own self rather than on the spiritual weapons of truth, righteousness, peace, faith, salvation and the Word of God.

There is a major difference between walking in our own intellect, will and emotion or walking in truth, righteousness, peace, faith, salvation and God's Word. The first we do in our own strength; the other we must do as fully submitted to the Lord and in His strength.

People do not like to change and they resist; that is just the way human nature is. We do not want to admit or accept that something may be wrong with the way we live or do things. *For us to be told we must develop virtue, holiness, character and worship in our life or to walk in truth, righteousness, peace, faith, salvation or God's Word, is really to say that, what we are doing now is not good enough.* For us as humans to be told we are not doing well enough does not make us feel good and it tends to create resistance.

Hindrances to Success

Come and let us reason together. *Is not the real problem with us in America that we are pretty well satisfied with ourselves?* What would happen if God wanted us to change something that we did not want to change? We would not likely be openly rebellious to God, but what happens to our total submission and obedience? What happens is resistance and rationalization.

How much rationalization have we done when we convince ourselves that God really does not want us to do whatever it is in our mind? How often do we convince ourselves it is our own idea and not God speaking to us? That is most often rationalization.

On the other hand, maybe it is someone else hinting or suggesting that we should change or should do something differently; surely, we think, that could not be God.

When we walk in the life-style that God teaches and when we come into His presence by following His pattern of the tabernacle, we then should know that it is God speaking to us when we get that little nudging in our conscience or that sense in the pit of our stomach.

When we learn to come into His presence, when we learn to ask for His leading and counsel, and when we are truly set on glorifying Him, then we can learn to have confidence in recognizing His voice. We recognize His voice because we have been in His presence, because we have spent time with Him in His Word and in prayer, and because we have had His voice confirmed by others or through some life situation.

How do we grow in godliness? Simply put, godliness is going the way God wants us to go. Godly behavior is modeled after Jesus Christ himself. We need to understand that our conduct is the most effective sermon we will ever preach. We must live our life in ways that will give consistent and undeniable evidence of the truth of

Christ's love and the truth of the Gospel.

A major aspect of holiness is living a life that is separated from the world; it is being set apart by God and being different from unbelievers. Of course, we live in the world but we are to be separated from the world and its pleasures and possessions.

The greatest battle the men have at Marion Correctional Institution is the battle with human nature. It is a battle we all have, it is just that outside the prison where we live it is easier to hide the flaws of our human nature. The lust of the eyes, the lust of the flesh and the pride of life are areas of the world that we all must deal with, especially those on the front lines of the battle for people's souls and for the soul of our cities.

How Do We Live Separated From The World?

Being holy is being pure and cleansed, dedicated to the service of God. We must be careful to avoid and reject the world's way of thinking. Without question, thinking as the world does will unavoidably lead to sensuality and impurity.

Of course, we must all live in the world, but how do we do that? How can we keep from being a part of the world and still be in the world, as we must?

We can be in the world and still buy the things we need, but we are not to be materialistic like the world.

We can be in the world and eat, but we are not to be gluttons and overeat like so many in America do.

We can be in the world and still work, but we are not to be workaholics like so many are in America.

We can be in the world and still play, but we are not to overemphasize recreation.

We can be in the world and have possessions, but we are not to hoard riches or allow what we have to become an idol for us.

We can be in the world and still have fellowship, but we are not to neglect duty.

If any of these issues, or any other issue not mentioned, should be a problem for you, they are issues to take before the Lord as you follow the tabernacle pattern. Have a conversation about the issue with the Lord beneath the wings of the cherubim at the mercy seat. ***When you do, know with certainty that the conversation that goes on in your mind or spirit is with the Lord.*** Any impressions you have will be certain to have come from Him if you have followed the pattern correctly. I emphasize, you must follow the pattern correctly, with 100% of your heart.

When we are learning to live in the presence of God and still live our daily life in the world, one of the greatest issues we will face will be with people. There can be plans, processes, procedures and programs, but for the most part the issues we face will usually involve people.

Our relationships are to be loving, truthful, selfless and submissive. We are to relate to others as Jesus relates to the Father and to us. We must practice honesty and truthfulness in all our relationships. We must deal with anger quickly and not allow it to influence our treatment of others. We must tame our tongue and avoid criticism, negative attitudes, destructive attitudes and any impure or immoral speech or behavior. This is all very clear in the pattern of behavior God has given us in Ephesians.

When we have God's divine order or pattern in place in our lives, we will have found the missing piece.

All that has been written in these last two chapters require that we have faith. We will turn to a discussion of faith and its meaning in the next chapter.

GOD'S PATTERN OF FAITH

REVIEW

We have seen in Part 2 how the pattern of the tabernacle represents God's prescribed way of entering into His presence. We have also seen from the chapter on the missing piece that it is essential to function in the presence of God in all we do.

We have seen from the Book of Ephesians just how God is sending us through boot camp to prepare us for war. We have seen that the preparation for that war is not the same preparation that the world makes for war; it is a preparation for warring through peace, which is done by how we conduct our daily life-style and live in the presence of the Lord.

The life-style preparation is to teach us how to make war against the enemy through peace.

We make war through peace by walking in truth, which is Jesus Christ.

We make war through peace by living righteous lives

so that we strive after the very righteousness of Jesus Christ.

We make war through peace by walking in peace, as much as it is our choice, always being ready to bear witness to the gospel.

We make war through peace by our faith in Jesus Christ—by a faith that He will protect us from the doubt and evil the enemy throws at us.

We make war through peace by protecting our minds with our salvation, knowing we are saved and have a glorious hope of eternal life.

We make war through peace by living in His Word, and learning to use the Word, as we free those people who are captive to the devil.

We make war through peace by praying in the Holy Spirit; that is, knowing we are in the Holy Spirit and the Holy Spirit is in us. Therefore, we pray in the Spirit and not in our own thoughts.

DESCRIPTION OF FAITH

We now need to turn our attention to the faith required for implementing and carrying out all we have been learning.

The Bible has much to say about faith, but Hebrews 11:1 is the only place that defines faith.

Learning to live by faith is the key to success for being able to live the life that prepares us to use the weapons of war and that prepares us to live in the presence of God.

Since Hebrews 11:1 is the only place in the Bible that we get a description of faith we need to look closely at what it says. *"Now faith is the substance of things hoped for, the evidence of things not seen."*

The word "substance" in the Greek means foundation, assurance, guarantee (of things hoped for) and title deed. The word "evidence" in the Greek means conviction.

If we look closely at what is being said in this definition of faith we see that ***faith is an act***. It is an act of our heart and mind in believing something and we have assurance and conviction that the something is true.

Again, if we look closely at what the Greek meaning is saying to us, we see that *faith is an actual possession of something.* When we have the title deed, when we have the guarantee of something, we actually possess that thing. Faith is actually the substance, the title deed assurance, of the actual possession. It is from the act of the mind and heart focusing on that substance hoped for—that is, focusing on the promise of God. The physical evidences of those promises are not yet actually seen, but because we have faith, we know the promises of God actually exist.

Let me give an example of what is being said here. If we were to buy something over the Internet (the thing not being physically seen or in our physical possession), and we paid for that item with a credit card, or by using Pay Pal, we would receive a receipt by email indicating the transaction was paid for and the item would be shipped sometime in the near future. We do not actually have possession of the item but we have proof of purchase or evidence of ownership, and that gives us title deed; it gives a guarantee of the item even though we have not yet taken actual possession. As a result, we actually own the item and it will soon be in our actual possession.

So, when the Bible's definition of faith says, *"Faith is the substance of things hoped for, the evidence of things not seen,"* we are to understand that with true faith and belief, we actually have ownership of the object of our faith even though we may not yet have actual possession. In other words, *when we have faith in God's Word, we have ownership of all God's promises, even though we may not yet have actual possession of those promises. Faith is more than an act; it is the actual possession of reality.*

Faith is actually possessing the substance of God's promises. Faith is the evidence of those promises that we have not yet put our eyes on. It is through faith that we know we already possess the promises; therefore, the substance of the promise is already there, that is, the evidence is there through our faith. Our faith is our receipt that we own the promises; they are actually ours.

We can say that faith is the substance, which is the actual possession, of the things we hoped for; that is, the evidence and the reality of the things we cannot yet see. We see that *faith is both an act and a possession of the thing we believe. We may not be able to see it, but it is real and it exists and it is ours, just like the example of the Internet purchase.*

Jesus Christ shed His blood for us to pay for our sins. He purchased our freedom from death. Faith is trusting, believing, having confidence in and possessing all that God is and says and has promised. Biblical faith knows what is real; it experiences and possesses what is real, and all God's promises are real.

THE ENCOURAGEMENT TO RUN THE RACE

According to the book of Hebrews, we have a whole host of witnesses who have run the race before us, and it is as if they are in the grandstand cheering us on as we run the race ourselves in this season. They have had success in running the race of faith and are now encouraging us, letting us know we can do it because they were people just like us and they did it. They are letting us know the kind of faith they exercised in order to run the race successfully. That way we can learn from them.

FAITH FOR US TO COPY

We need to look now at the kind of faith each of our predecessors had when they were running their race. In doing that, *we can learn from their successes.*

We must train ourselves to have the mindset of faith—the mindset of expectation and belief—to have a winning attitude. *How successful we are in training ourselves to have this mindset of expectation and belief will determine how successful we will be in exercising our faith.*

As we train in boot camp for the war, a major part of our training is self-discipline; what better way to practice self-discipline than to prepare ourselves for a race.

We can, and must, grow in the strength and power of our faith. We can do this by practicing hope. That is, by hoping for what God has promised because He knows what is best and has put the promises in His Word.

We can also grow in faith and power by hungering and thirsting after righteousness; by continually asking, seeking and knocking; by first seeking His kingdom and His righteousness; by persevering in prayer and by fasting.

Able and **Enoch** had a *faith with spiritual power. Their faith had the spiritual power to be counted as righteousness by God, and they exercised the power to walk day by day in the presence of God.*

Able believed God and approached Him exactly as directed. Enoch also believed God and walked and fellowshipped day by day with God.

Both Able and Enoch knew what is said in Hebrews 11:6 *"But without faith it is impossible to please God: for he that cometh to God must believe that He is, and that He is a rewarder of them that diligently seek Him."*

Without faith, a person will never be acceptable to God or will never live with God. Without faith, we have to struggle through life, and try to solve all the trials and temptations that come our way by ourselves. We stand alone in the world.

We must believe that God exists and that He is a rewarder of those who seek Him with all (100%) of their heart.

Noah had a faith that was *fearful and reverent toward God. He was so sure of the existence of God that he feared disobeying Him out of a godly, reverent fear.*

Noah was mocked and ridiculed by the world, yet he stood in awe of who God was and of His warning.

God is going to judge the earth and all mankind again, and we need to believe Him and fear Him with such a godly fear and reverence that what others say or think makes no difference. We must be in awe of who He is and heed His Word as we diligently seek Him.

Abraham had a faith that was *obedient and hopeful. God called Abraham and he was obedient to the call; he believed God. Even though he did not know where he was going, Abraham went; he had no map and no destination. He just believed the promises of God and he acted on the hope of those promises.*

Abraham also had *a sacrificial faith* in that he obeyed God regardless of the cost. In the case of Isaac it was the possible death of his beloved son. It was the ultimate faith for Abraham to sacrifice Isaac.

We must learn from this to trust God and to love Him above all else. We must believe God's promises, even when we see no way they can take place and we cannot understand what He is asking.

Sarah had a faith that *believed the impossible.* She believed God that she would have a child even when it was humanly impossible for her at 90 years of age. *At first, Sarah did not believe the promise of a child at her age, but when she considered that God was the God and creator of the universe, she believed.* Because she believed the impossible, God gave her the impossible.

Isaac had a faith that was *a repentant faith. Isaac believed the promises of God but he needed to repent from his own willful decision* to give Esau the family blessing rather that Jacob, as God had declared.

Jacob had a faith that was a *worshiping faith.* Even though Jacob never saw the Promised Land that God had promised His people, and was sent into captivity in Egypt instead, *he never stopped believing and worshiping God right up to his death.*

Joseph had a faith that was an *undying faith.* *He believed despite very difficult circumstances.* He believed without any doubt that God was going to fulfill His promises. He believed that God was going to give the Promised Land, and he believed that God had chosen his family to be the bloodline to the promised Seed of the Messiah.

Moses had a faith that was *a self-denying faith.* He had all that life could offer in worldly terms, but he gave it all up. *He sacrificed everything because he believed God's promises of the promised Seed and the Promised Land.*

Moses also had *an expectant faith* in that *he gave up all that Egypt had to offer and deliberately made the decision to suffer with his people and to inherit the promises made by God.*

GOD'S PROMISE TO US TODAY

How do we get to the place of the patriarchs in our faith today? We have more evidence available to us today than the cloud of witnesses had. We still have the Creation and God's Word as they had, but we also have the life of Jesus to study; we have the book of Revelation, which is God's specific message to us about what is going to happen in the end times; and we have the work of the Holy Spirit living in us.

All of the cloud of witnesses who came before us, those encouraging us to run the race to win, had in common their belief in the promises of God. Those promises they each held to, were those of believing in the Promised Land and in the promised Seed, Jesus Christ.

Today, the promised Seed has already come, in the form of Jesus Christ. He has paid the price for our being able to be freed from sin and being able to spend eternity in the Promised Land of heaven.

This is God's will; this is what God is doing today. He is calling people to faith and belief in the new promised land of heaven and the return of His Seed, Jesus Christ, who will make a new heaven and a new earth.

We today must develop the different kinds of faith exhibited by the patriarchs of days gone by. We must believe and hold to the promises of God that His Seed will return and there will be a new heaven and a new earth—our Promised Land. *The Promised Land of heaven and the return of the promised Seed of Jesus to earth are still before us. This is our great hope. This promise we should be willing to die for.*

WHAT STANDS IN THE WAY OF OUR FAITH?

Matthew 17: 14-21 gives us the answer to this question. When Jesus came down from the Mount of Transfiguration, a man approached Him for help because he had a young, demon-possessed son, and Jesus' disciples had not been able to cast out the demon.

The ministry of the disciples was powerless to help the child. The very persons who should have been able to help were the disciples. Nine disciples were there when the child's father first came for help, yet none of them was able to deliver the boy.

It is clear from Jesus' answer to the disciples' question as to why they were unable to cast out the demon that it was because of their unbelief. *The clear question before us is what causes our faith to weaken and turn into unbelief? What causes unbelief?*

Unbelief is doubting Christ; it is questioning in ourselves whether Christ is strong enough to deal with evil in the world, to deal with evil nations or to do what is needed.

Unbelief is doubting ourselves, by doubting whether we really have Christ in us. It is questioning whether we are close enough to Christ for Him to hear us or for Him to think He can trust us enough to give us the power needed.

Unbelief is doubting our own faith. It is questioning whether we are close enough to Christ to be dependent on Him and to have the confidence in our relationship with Him.

Unbelief is questioning whether what we ask is really God's will. It is questioning if we should really be seeking such a thing, or it is questioning if God is willing to do what we believe is needed.

Unbelief is having a sense that Christ is far away and out of reach, and the indwelling presence and power of Christ just cannot be identified.

Unbelief is caused by a lack of leadership, when that lack causes the faith and loyalty of some to weaken. The nine disciples apparently had no leader to demonstrate faith and power for them when they were trying to cast the demon out of the young boy. Their leader, Jesus, was on the mountain-top.

Unbelief can be caused by an atmosphere of questioning. This often affects the faith and power of a person's life. Many of those present around the disciples as they worked with the young boy created an atmosphere of unbelief and distrust in God as the disciples unsuccessfully attempted to cast out the demon.

It is important to note that when Christians have *no power* it affects their testimony. The world uses the lives of believers to judge not only their testimony about Christ and Christianity, but to judge Christ Himself. The world tries to discredit Christ because of the powerlessness of believers.

What is the answer to unbelief? We must hunger and thirst after God so desperately that we seek to spend a great deal of time in His presence, so desperate for Him that we even forget about eating, and we will go without food to seek Him.

PRAYER AND FASTING

When the disciples asked Jesus why they were unable to cast the demon out of the child, Jesus told them something else besides having a lack of faith. He told them that the particular kind of demon they were dealing with goes out only by prayer and fasting. *Now this is interesting, because Jesus did not stop to pray and fast before casting out the demon.*

What was going on? Jesus lived a life-style of prayer and fasting. He would arise early each morning and go up into the mountain to pray, and it is assumed, to also fast. He was in the presence of the Father constantly. He prayed so fervently and diligently that He forgot about eating, so He was ready with power for whatever He saw the Father doing before Him.

The disciples had not recognized that Jesus received power through prayer, by being in the presence of God, and by fasting. That is why Jesus was impatient with them. He was modeling and living out what they needed to be doing themselves, but they were not learning.

Prayer is one of the greatest acts of the Christian believer. Talking to God, whether by thought or by tongue, is the way a believer fellowships with Him. One thing God desires is fellowship with man. Thus, it is essential that we pray and pray often, sharing and fellowshipping with Him all day long.

Fasting is going without food for some religious purpose. However, it is more than just going without food. It is being so consumed with a situation that the situation becomes more important than food, so the believer sets food aside to become consumed with seeking God about the situation. It is doing without food in order to concentrate on God and His answer to the particular matter.

Fasting for recognition, for reward or for religious duty is wrong, and will not be honored by God. However, we are told to fast and, as believers, we are expected to fast. So what is the correct way?

Fasting is to be done without notice. We are not to let others know we are seeking God in a very special way over an important situation.

Fasting is to be to God alone. We are to diligently seek only Him and be dependent only on Him.

We should fast when we feel a special pull on our heart to get alone with God. There are times when special needs arise and we need to fast over the situation.

We should also fast when we sense a need to humble ourselves before God, as well as at times when we need a very special power from God. This could be at times when we believe we will be faced with opportunities to minister. If the disciples had been in the habit of praying and fellowshipping with God all through the day and fasting on a regular basis for the power to minister, they would not have been powerless when faced with a child in need.

CONCLUSION TO PART TWO

In the second part of this book, we have seen the pattern God has provided for us to come into His presence and how Jesus Christ represents for us today each of those steps in the tabernacle. It is only through Jesus Christ that we can approach the presence of God.

We have seen how the book of Ephesians lays out a life-style for us to live and to prepare us for the spiritual war we are in.

We have seen how our witnesses from the past have given us models of how to apply our faith and how they are examples of encouragement to us today.

We have also seen how faith, prayer and fasting give us power to use the armor of our spiritual weapons. We have seen how truth, righteousness, peace, faith, salvation, the Word of God and prayer are the spiritual weapons used for living our everyday life in warfare with the devil and his demons.

Hebrews 11:1 (NLT)

What is faith? It is the confident assurance that what we hope for is going to happen. It is the evidence of things we cannot yet see.

PART 3
ISSUES

Introduction to Part 3

This part is somewhat technical and represents a dramatic change of pace in the flow of the book. The material contained here will be of interest to those in leadership and those responsible for the smooth flow of relationships in the city-reaching efforts.

However, for the busy person who participates in city-reaching efforts on a part time basis, these three chapters could be skipped without missing the purpose or flow of the book.

The content of this part deals with issues of putting together a city-reaching movement, dealing with relationships as people work together in groups and understanding how people use power and influence as a part of who they are.

Having a good grip on the basics of these three chapters would be quite beneficial to leaders of city-transformation efforts.

1 John 1:8-10 (NLT)

If we say we have no sin, we are only fooling ourselves and refusing to accept the truth. [9]But if we confess our sins to him, he is faithful and just to forgive us and to cleanse us from every wrong. [10]If we claim we have not sinned, we are calling God a liar and showing that his word has no place in our hearts.

ISSUES

INTRODUCTION

Our thinking must be clear on several critical issues if we are to expect success at transforming our cities.

It would be unreasonable to expect that everyone reading this book will agree on all these concepts, but it is expected that reason will prevail and the obvious will be recognized. The obvious is that what we have been doing has not produced a city in America that is well on its way to being transformed. After well over fifteen years of serious effort, success has continued to evade us. Therefore, reason dictates that we do some serious re-evaluation of our approach.

In this chapter, we will consider some critical issues that are sometimes very subtle, but none-the-less need to be addressed.

TERMINOLOGY

The need for a standard vocabulary is a critical issue

that will need to be addressed before we are able to develop transferable methodologies in city-reaching. It is not the intent in this book to address that need.

However, let us look for a moment at how some terms are used in this book. I am not attempting to establish new definitions or language for community transformation, but only to describe the meaning of terms as they are meant to be understood here.

CITY—The term **city** is defined as the inhabitants of the city collectively. Therefore, when we talk about transforming a city, we are talking about transforming the inhabitants of that city. In addition, when we are talking about city-reaching, we are talking about reaching the inhabitants of the city in such a way that their lives are changed for the better because of Jesus Christ.

CHURCH—The term **church** needs to be defined when it is used because of so many different meanings, none of which is wrong. The reference to the word becomes very confusing, and when one is reading various city-reaching materials, one tends to put in the definition that suits the topic. This leads to diverse meanings in the minds of different readers.

According to New Unger's Bible Dictionary, the term church is used to express different ideas, and it lists five ways in which the word is used. It is used to signify: (1) the entire body of those who are saved by their relation to Christ, (2) a particular Christian denomination, (3) the aggregate of all the ecclesiastical communions professing faith in Christ, (4) a single organized Christian group and (5) a building designated for Christian worship [1.]

For the purpose of this book, the word church will not be used by itself, but will always have a descriptor to clarify its meaning.

TRANSFORMATION AND CITY-REACHING—The terms **transformation and city-reaching** are used synonymously in this book.

Transformation means to undergo a change in form; this change in form may be that of character change, attitude change, physical change, spiritual change or structural change. City-reaching and transformation mean that the transformation will more and more lead to, or be able to be done in, an atmosphere where Christ is increasingly welcome.

Community Transformation—The term **community transformation** will mean in this book, social, political, economic and spiritual change in a climate where Christ is increasingly welcome. It makes sense that not everything will change at the same time; therefore, we need to establish criteria for identifying and measuring the change.

Several ways of identifying and measuring change may be done by using the Otis Scale for community assessment, spiritual mapping information, police reports, economic reports and education reports. Change may also be measured by follow-up responses from government, education and business leaders to the question of "What are the problems you are facing for which you have no effective solution?" As the intercessors focus specific prayer for a solution to those problems, a comparison may be made of the before and after prayer results.

Persevering Leadership

There are two kinds of persevering leadership being considered here. One is the kind of persevering leadership that assesses where we are, how successful we have been, and then makes adjustments where necessary—even if the adjustments are in the foundational structure of our efforts. The leaders involved here are creative and are also builders. They make the time commitment to pursue success in changing the spiritual climate of their city.

The other kind of persevering leadership is the kind that has blinders on to the fact that we are stuck and are not having much success in city-reaching—yet, they continue to press forward with the same old programs or mindsets. The leaders involved here are not careless, or thoughtless. For the most part, they are very busy people who are looking for a formula to plug into rather than reinventing the wheel. ***A hope of this book is to help the leader*** *who does not have the time to do much foundation building, but is able to get some basic principles in place.*

Persevering leadership is a two-edged sword. We can persevere because we are sold out to the Lord's will, or we can persevere because it is something we ourselves can do by exercising our own leadership skills and by determining with our own self-will to make something work.

George Otis found four common factors[2] existing in all third-world countries that were being transformed, one of which was persevering leadership. When we look at Otis's factor of persevering leadership, and we add to it the American perspective of doing work rather than of being in the presence of God, we lose something profoundly important. *We lose the third-world perspective of being in the presence of God*. We have already discussed the absolute necessity of balance between being in God's presence and of doing work for God.

I am not at all implying that we forget about doing the work. We must come to that, and we must do the work at some point. However, we must first be in His presence and we must learn to be there on a continuing basis. Doing this is a mark of the kingdom person.

KINGDOM PEOPLE

When we run into kingdom people, we know there is something different about them. They are godly people determined to do the will of God even when it is not the popular thing to do.

There are more of these kingdom people than we might expect and they are seeking to find each other. They are attempting to identify one another and to hook up with one another. They all have a gifting from God, and that gifting dramatically meshes with the gifting of others. They are learning to recognize that gifting, and they are recognizing the need for all the parts in the body to come together to make the whole that God desires.

These kingdom people are kingdom builders and not empire builders. *These kingdom people clearly see the*

war we are in and know it is a spiritual war. They
see how the enemy stalks after people and how he steals
life. They see how he places people in bondage, and how
he kills and destroys the lives of people. As kingdom builders, they see clearly that the role God has placed them in
is a role that will carry on the mission of Christ. They
know Christ has passed His ministry on to them. They
know they are responsible for carrying out the ministry
He spoke in Luke 4:18-19. There He said, *"The Spirit of
the Lord is upon Me, because He has anointed Me to preach
the gospel to the poor; He has sent Me to heal the broken-
hearted, to proclaim liberty to the captives and recovery of
sight to the blind, to set at liberty those who are oppressed;
to proclaim the acceptable year of the Lord."*

The Luke 4:18-19 scripture is the heartbeat of kingdom people and they view all church congregations and
ministers as partners in carrying out that role.

Kingdom people know they are in the world but not of
the world. They know they are to eat but not be gluttons.
They know they need money and have to work, but they
are not greedy. They know they have to have things from
the world to get along, but they are not materialistic. They
know they need exercise, recreation and relaxation, but
they are not self-indulgent. In short, they take care of
their mental, physical and spiritual health so they will be
more effective as witnesses and as workers for the Lord.

We are inspired by the kingdom people and are eager
to be a part of what they are doing; they are authentic and
unselfish.

EMPIRE PEOPLE

The empire builders on the other hand, view life and
ministry from their own perspective; that is, from inside
themselves. They are absorbed with how well they do,
how they look, how they are seen by others, how well they
compete, how successful they are in the sight of the world,
how many programs they have, how large their ministry
is, how much money they have. They see other local
churches as competitors. *They are often self-indulgent*

and self-focused. They often have vision and success that is envied by the world.

The empire person leaves us with a knot in our stomachs and we know there is just "something" there that makes us a little uncomfortable, something that is just not quite right, that is, unless we are also in the world ourselves.

The empire people have all the right words and speak all the right ideas and beliefs, but while they are talking their talk, we pick up little clues in their words, life or behavior, that tip us off that something is just not authentic.

Let us face it—some of the people who become involved in community transformation are empire builders, and are usually attracted to the endeavor for the opportunities it provides to demonstrate and promote their own ministry or their own agenda.

Fortunately, the empire people are a minority in community transformation and are somewhat offset by the kingdom builders. However, if they ever get in charge, or become influencers, the project is headed for trouble.

We must remember it is the nature of empire people to attempt to become influencers or be in charge. We must also remember that for God to be involved, He must be the one to receive glory and not man.

The empire builder may or may not be a carnal person. The empire person could very well be a true believer who has pinpointed his own portion of Nehemiah's wall that he is going to build. His pride will compel him to build it better than anyone else has ever done.

The problem then is the competition the empire people have with others and their focus on the reason they are building. Unfortunately, the empire builders tend to be very competitive at the expense of outdoing others, or sometimes even running over others.

The empire builder faces the extreme danger of eventually taking glory from God and applying it to the empire he has built or is building.

It is difficult for empire people to drop their own

agenda and to divert their resources and energies to the city as a whole, especially to an area which does not benefit their own agenda.

Empire people we run into in city-reaching efforts are usually carnal Christians. However, some empire people have never accepted Christ as their Savior. They simply call themselves Christian because they attend some local church; there are even some people in positions of pastor who have never accepted Christ as their Savior and who believe only parts of the Bible. They are Christian in name only and therefore cannot even be considered carnal Christians, which we will discuss next.

We need to learn to identify and deal with both empire builders and carnal Christians.

CARNAL PEOPLE

One of the difficult issues we must face is having available to us that very good person who knows everybody worth knowing in the city, who is well respected in the city, who wields tremendous influence in the city, and yet who is carnal and spiritually immature and has been for many, many years. This is a difficult issue because we are tempted to permit that person to hold a core leadership position in our city-reaching efforts.

The carnal Christian is different from the person who is a new Christian and has just recently come to the Lord.

We have no way of knowing the heart and the inner struggle the new Christian person is going through with the Lord. However, we can expect to see some effort and some evidence of change over time in the character and behavior of that new Christian.

On the other hand, the carnal Christians live in the flesh and at the human level of life. The change expected in the character and behavior, over time, is just not observable. They allow their flesh to dominate and control their behavior.

Carnal people are usually people professing to be Christian, but just have not given up the things of the world. We have to face it—our church buildings are full of carnal Christians on any given Sunday.

It is extremely unfortunate that most carnal Christians are not held accountable for their carnal behavior by church leadership. They are allowed to believe that their life-style and behavior is acceptable for Christians.

In 1 Corinthians 3:1-3, Paul tells the Corinthians that they belong to the world and they are carnal, fleshly, controlled by their own sinful desires, and they are unspiritual. Paul is saying they were mere human beings, made of flesh. They were still living at the human level of life and had not gotten beyond the affairs and material things of this world.

The Corinthians acted as though this world was all there was and the flesh dominated them. They were allowing the flesh and its possessions to control their behavior.

The understanding about the carnal man is extremely important for us today as we bring the Kingdom of God into our city. We must be able to distinguish between those persons who are new Christians and who are still trying to overcome all the bad habits of their sinful lives and those persons who profess to be Christians and yet who have shown no signs over time of changing from their worldly lives to follow Christ.

We need to be careful that the professing carnal Christians do not determine spiritual guidelines for our coming into the presence of God; they simply do not know how. Those people will invariably have talents, abilities and influence that could be very helpful in our city-reaching endeavors. However, God will bring the core leadership people alongside that He wants to be with us. We do not need to be impressed by the world's highly qualified people.

The carnal man is not spiritually mature. Note that the carnal man is a believer, but he has continued to remain a babe in Christ. He should be more mature, more developed spiritually—but he has not grown, over time, in Christ. The carnal man does not know Christ and the things of God as he should. His mind and behavior are not focused upon Christ as they should be. He may have been a believer for years, but he knows little about Christ and God.

The carnal man feeds on the milk of the Word and not on the meat of the Word. The same gospel is preached to all, and all study the same Word; but some have paid attention, studied, prayed, meditated on the Word and served Christ more than others. Therefore, they naturally know more about God's Word, and know more about what it means to pray and walk in Christ.

The true believer has learned more, knows more and experiences more of the depth of spiritual things than the carnal believer. The carnal believer has to be fed the very basics over and over, and never gets to the depths of God's Word.

The same is true with any endeavor of man. The more a person experiences and studies a field, the more he knows his field. Everyone feeds on either the "milk" or the "meat" of his field or endeavor.

Division characterizes the carnal man. Division is striking proof of the carnality of a man or of a group of people, whether the division is in a church group, in a family or in the work place.

Carnality is clearly seen in envy and strife. Envy leads to jealousy, and jealousy leads to division. When people become jealous of one another they become divided, and they begin to strive against one another and to argue and bicker with one another.

Causes of envy could be such things as position, recognition, promotion, possession, gift, wealth, attention or some person. The list could go on and on, but the point is clear: envy leads to differences and strife, and strife leads to division. Such behavior is of the flesh and is an example of carnality. It does not belong in the core leadership of the city-reaching endeavor, or the core leadership of the church group for that matter.

Carnality is seen when believers walk and act like men of the world. Men of the world live for the world, so they want, and struggle for, all they can get. They want, and struggle for, the best position, the most money, the coveted possession, the highest honor and the most recognition.

Carnality is seen when believers begin to follow men and begin to form cliques.

The core leadership must come into the presence of God and develop relationship with one another. *There must be commitment and relationship, in the presence of God, among the core leadership.* Until they, as a corporate body, have the strength of that position in Christ, they are vulnerable to being diluted and compromised by the carnal.

If we are going to see our community transformed, we have to recognize that it has to be God that does it and not man. That is the case for the missing piece. We must come into, and stay in, the presence of God until He sends us to work and we have assurance that He goes with us, and that we do not go in our own strength.

INCLUSIVENESS

This brings us to the topics of inclusion, selective inclusion during the organizational stage, and exclusion. How do we deal with this? How can we be inclusive and not be controlled by the empire builders or by the carnal people?

The current thinking in city-reaching is that there must be inclusion and that it takes the whole church to reach the whole city. It has to be assumed that what is meant by the whole church here is everyone in all the different church buildings in the city.

We must strive for inclusiveness in the city-reaching efforts. That must be a goal toward which to work.

If inclusion of everyone in all the different churches is the meaning of the current thinking, and I believe it is, then we must plan for, and overcome, a concern that, if not dealt with, can sabotage the city-reaching efforts. *The concern is that both empire builders and carnal Christians will bring the world's ways with them when they are included.*

I understand that some efforts at city-reaching have outside consultants who come in and help organize, assign leadership, and move pastors and ministry leaders toward reconciliation and repentance. This is a good thing to do, and has to help, but not all city-reaching efforts have that luxury. Therefore, those that do not have this luxury must be acutely aware of the dangers here to the success of their mission.

I would point out here that the MCI model has clearly shown that *not every participant in the transformation effort needs to be Christian;* participation allowed for a non-threatening entry point for involvement. That non-threatening opportunity to participate eventually drew many of those participating non-Christians to Christ.

SELECTIVE INCLUSION

We must strive for inclusiveness, but we must start with selective inclusiveness for a core leadership group. That is, we must start with leadership that is willing to spend time together building relationship in the presence of the Lord, and building a core leadership team.

What is meant by selective inclusion is that the core leadership team must be developed separately at the very beginning. Selective inclusion must be used to establish the foundational core leadership for the city-reaching effort.

There must be a willingness on the part of the core leadership team to commit whatever time it takes to come corporately into the presence of God, while at the same time build relationship with one another by spending time together.

Unity with God and with one another is critical for the core leadership. There must be a genuine consensus among all involved in the relationship-building process on how it will be determined when God says it is time to go and time to do.

I say genuine consensus because leadership within the group must be allowed to emerge. If there are those in the group who hold leadership positions in the world, they will naturally tend to assert that leadership. When they do, others will tend to yield to it.

If any of those who are leaders in the marketplace tend to be action-oriented, it is easy for them to subtly lead others in the direction of moving before it is really in God's will that the group should move, so an understanding of having consensus is essential.

CORE LEADERSHIP

God's chosen leadership must emerge, and those who like being leaders, or who are accustomed to being leaders, must willingly yield and be a supporting partner to those God chooses.

The core leadership team must be willing to devote the time to develop relationship with others on the core team. They must be willing to seek the presence of the presiding Jesus and seek His will and guidance for the core team and for the city.

Those who really desire to be included in the core leadership team must be willing to submit to the Lord and to each other. They must also be willing to invest the time and energy to develop close, meaningful relationships with each other, and corporately, with Jesus Christ.

In the early stages of formation of the core leadership team and their direction and strategy development, there must be selective inclusion. This dedicated core group of kingdom people will come together, and will come into the presence of God as they humble themselves, pray fervently, seek His face and turn from their sins. They need to follow God's prescribed pattern for doing that, and they need to stay in God's presence until there is agreement that He has released them and shown them how to proceed.

If being released and sent to work by God takes three weeks, three months or three years, the core group must obey and persevere. The problem is we do not believe anyone will commit that kind of time to wait for the leading of the Lord, especially leaders. Because of our unbelief, we tend to cut the time short. When we do that, we have moved in our timing and not God's. Any success would be the result of our timing, and we would receive glory instead of God receiving it. We already know God will not permit anyone to share His glory.

RELATIONSHIPS

Building relationships is the key to sustaining involvement of the core leadership group. *People have to get to know each other and to trust and care for each other. People have to spend time together.*

The relationships of the core leadership, once developed, will lead to corporately coming into the presence of God and confessing, repenting and reconciling to one another.

After coming to the place in relationship where the core group can corporately and humbly seek God and come into His presence together, He will reveal to the group the vision for the city, or for the church. This will lead to organizational and strategic planning to fulfill His vision. All this will then be in God's proper timing.

The organizational structure will accomplish the vision because that vision will have come from God, and because people care for each other and see value in their unity and value in participating together.

Relationship involves more than just a vision; it involves our commitment to people we know and trust.

EXCLUSIVENESS

There is little to be said here. The avoidance of exclusiveness is necessary. As we have seen in the MCI model, there are men who are not Christian believers, and many of the men belong to different faiths. There is an open invitation to them to participate, and they certainly do enjoy the benefits of a changed and much safer environment.

If those of different faiths or non-believers at MCI had felt they were being excluded, it could have been a very testy and dangerous situation. Rather, they have enjoyed more freedom to practice their own faith, even when their choice was to have no faith.

At the same time, selective inclusion for establishing core leadership made it possible to establish a firm leadership foundation. That firm foundation made it possible for the spiritual climate to be changed and for the prison to experience transformation.

A WAY TO BE INCLUSIVE

We need a way to be inclusive and yet separate out from leadership those who would dilute our continual efforts to be in the presence of God.

The following is adapted from Ted Haggard's book *Primary Purpose*[3] and from other thoughts. *It gives us guidelines for dealing with the critical issue of what people believe and how we align ourselves with the different beliefs that are out there.*

Haggard identifies different bases for a person's beliefs which he calls absolutes, interpretations, deductions, subjective opinions, personal preferences, feelings and cultural norms.

The following descriptions of those bases of belief provide a firm foundation for a broad cross-section of the Christian community to join in a city transformation effort.

Absolutes—Everyone must agree on the absolutes. Absolutes include the following facts: that Jesus is God; that Jesus was born of the Virgin Mary; that Jesus rose from the dead; that He ascended into heaven; that salvation comes only through Christ; that there is only one true God manifested in three, God the Father, God the Son and God the Holy Spirit; that Jesus is coming again; that sin separates us from eternal life; that it is only through Jesus we have access to the Father; that the Bible is our only primary source of information about God and Jesus Christ; and that the written expression of the absolutes of the Ten Commandments is still our guide today.

Absolutes are not subject to personal convictions, cultural trends, feelings or interpretations. They are the same at anytime in any society. Sins of the past are still sins today, such as believing in and worshiping other gods, using God's name in vain, not keeping the Sabbath holy, dishonoring our parents, murder, sexual immorality, stealing, and lying.

We can never sacrifice an absolute. We must never waiver from our position here. Local churches that accept the absolutes can get together for prayer, fellowship and joint efforts. Examples of this are Promise Keepers, Christian concerts, days of prayer and joint community projects. We all must agree on the absolutes; this is core.

Interpretations—Next on the list, resting on the foundation of absolutes, are interpretations. These are scriptures, upon which we form opinions or sometimes even doctrines. They are always taken within the context of the passage. They are focused ideas, but since they are interpretations, there can sometimes be disagreement. The problem is when we allow this disagreement to divide us.

Examples of interpretations can be: everybody is meant to speak in tongues, pre-tribulation rapture, etc. Since these are not absolutes, it is all right to disagree. It is tragic when people deem certain movements and people as "false teachers" because they disagree with them over interpretation.

Deductions—Deductions are broader and more general than interpretations. You can arrive at a deduction when you read a larger portion of several passages of scripture. A deduction may be that sanctification is gradual rather than immediate.

Doctrines should never be made on deduction alone, but there is much liberty to allow your ministry to include deductions as long as they agree with and enhance the absolutes. As with interpretations, it is certainly negative to identify deductions as un-biblical when they in fact do not contradict an absolute.

Subjective Opinions—Broader still, subjective opinions are arrived at by individuals who experience certain insight when searching the scriptures, coupled with living out what they find. Of course, subjective opinions must always agree with absolutes and must not contradict scripture, or they must be thrown out.

Subjective opinions may include teaching that hymns are more effective than contemporary worship music, or that we should dress like the culture that we are trying to minister to and relate to them on their level. This is where ministry style can have a lot of freedom to experiment by trial and error. Discovering what works best in your situation at this level should never be accepted as absolute truth, or even as a deduction.

Personal Preferences—Personal preferences may have less to do with controversial scriptural matters and more to do with personality, likes and dislikes. For example, a minister may prefer to have a robed choir every Sunday while another may prefer a single barefoot guitar-playing worship leader straight out of the 70s. Another example would be to take tithes and offerings by passing a plate rather than having the congregation bring the tithe to the front of the sanctuary and lay it on the altar. The Bible is usually silent on such preferences.

Feelings—Feelings would include simply what we like and do not like. Can you believe there have been local church splits on this level over such things as what color the carpet should be, or whether to use hymnals or a video projector? Feelings have more to do with atmosphere than with anything else.

Cultural Norms—This simply has to do with the style and system of a particular culture. For example, you may find loud "Amen's!" in an Afro-American church service while it may be more subdued in another style of church service. We will also find a lot of cultural differences between different denominations and different socio-economic classes. If every church congregation were a hooting and hollering roller-coaster ride, then there would be a large segment of society who would not be reached, and vice versa.

ESSENTIALS

If we would just focus on the absolutes and resist creating divisions over nonessentials, we would have a powerful army ready and equipped to accomplish the Great Commission.

We need to encourage, and be in favor of, discussion because iron sharpens iron. However, sometimes the scripture remains silent or vague. As long as we do everything we can to create healthy relationships, healthy church congregations and healthy city-reaching endeavors, we have a lot of freedom to work.

As we reach out to others of different denominations and local churches, and as we prepare ourselves for His purposes, we must be able to take comfort in the fact that we agree on absolutes. We will then also be able to take comfort in allowing others the right of interpretation and of deduction without allowing those differences to divide us.

Matthew 28:18-20 (NLT)

Jesus came and told his disciples, "I have been given complete authority in heaven and on earth. [19]Therefore, go and make disciples of all the nations, baptizing them in the name of the Father and the Son and the Holy Spirit. [20]Teach these new disciples to obey all the commands I have given you. And be sure of this: I am with you always, even to the end of the age."

INTRODUCTION

The world has its own unique way of dealing with groups, power and influence. As Christians, we are not to model our behavior after the world. However, we are called to live in the world so it is necessary to understand how it operates. We all know that associating and dealing with people of the world is unavoidable in any city-reaching effort.

It is a fact that we have to associate with people of the world, as well as carnal Christians in the church. That, I believe, makes it necessary to present the material in the next two chapters.

POWER, INFLUENCE AND AUTHORITY

God has chosen leadership for reaching the city and they must be allowed to emerge. When that leadership does emerge, it may well be persons different from whom we would expect.

Those persons who like being leaders, or are accustomed to being leaders, but who are not chosen by God for this particular assignment, must willingly yield and be a supporting partner to those that emerge as God's chosen.

It is essential that God put together the leadership team. This can be threatening for those who think they should be leaders but are not selected by God for this particular assignment.

Power, influence and authority are critical factors that must be discussed when it comes to establishing core group relationships and the core leadership that will guide a diversity of people in the city into community transformation.

A distinction between power and authority needs to be understood. If we picture a Mack truck coming down the street, that Mack truck would represent power. At the same time, if there is a petite policewoman directing traffic and she holds up her hand to the Mack truck to stop, that truck will stop. The petite policewoman represents authority. The Mack truck is stronger and much more powerful than the petite policewoman, but she has authority to stop the powerful Mack.

A person who has power may not have authority, but the person who has authority has a special kind of power. In like manner, a person who has power may not have influence, but a person who has influence has a special kind of power.

There are people who, by their very demeanor, exude authority. It is expressed by their direct eye contact, by their handshake, by the confidence that is expressed in their conversation, by their easy smile, by how they carry themselves and by their positive and confident tone. These people may hold leadership positions or they may not, but they are the kind of leaders community transformation needs.

It is important to recognize that the issue of power, influence and authority is present in all relationship dynamics, whether in the family, the church, the social environment or the work environment. This is a subject we do not like to discuss. However, the issue exists and the dynamics must be taken into consideration. It is an uncomfortable subject and is therefore often avoided in emerging relationships.

Two things need to be addressed. First, the growth of the group that is, or will be, leading the community transformation efforts and second, the basis of power and influence that is asserted within that group.

This chapter will cover group growth, and in the next chapter, power and influence will be covered.

GROUP GROWTH MODEL

No community is going to be reached without like minds and hearts coming together. It is in the coming together where problems have arisen in past efforts at reaching cities. *The interaction between people is what will make or break the effort to bring the presence of God into the city.* Bringing the Kingdom of God into a city is done collectively by joining in unity those hearts already filled with the Holy Spirit, and by fervent and united prayer.

The coming together of people means that people have to get along and be more than just tolerant of one another. When issues of power, of influence, of authority, and of leadership collide and group growth becomes hindered, eventually the effort to reach the city fails.

First we will look at group growth through the model know as COG's Ladder.[1] This was named after its founder George O. Charrier and uses his initials backwards.

Any group of individuals working together will be more successful if they understand and apply the steps or phases in this model. It is a model of how the interactions work between people striving to come into some kind of relationship.

In working and relating together, all effective groups go through five stages or phases. When these stages are out of order the relationship and effectiveness of the group is hindered.

Many pastors and leaders have come together

with high hopes of changing their city but they never progress past the first two stages. As a result, there is discouragement, disappointment and eventually the effort just fades away.

PURPOSE OF THE GROUP MODEL PROCESS

We cannot operate in isolation as we attempt to bring the Kingdom of God to our city. We must interact with others and much of that interaction will be in groups. As we seek to come into the presence of God we must learn to practice coming into his presence corporately as well as individually.

It would be nice if all we had to worry about was our own relationship with the Lord. Unfortunately, Satan and his demons are at work and they definitely work through people. Therefore, as we attempt to come together to corporately change our church or our city, we need to know what to expect from the group we are working with. That way we will be better aware of the schemes of the enemy when he attempts to enter into our group relationships.

A summary of the five steps in group growth are as follows. First, is the polite, get acquainted stage. Second, is the searching for a purpose stage; it is asking, "Why are we here?" Third is the bid for power phase. If the group is able to grow past the third stage it will move into a cooperative and constructive fourth stage. Finally, the group will move into the fifth stage and develop a strong feeling of unity and *esprit de corps*, or a sense of oneness and of common purpose among group members.

Models of human behavior are, of necessity, simplistic in that we are unable to duplicate the interaction of the complexity of the human being; however, models do help us conceptualize abstract relationships.

It will be constructive to do a more detailed analysis of this particular model to help us conceptualize just how the dynamics would evolve as a core leadership group launches out to reach its city.

EXTREME CAUTION

An extreme caution is in order before learning about this model. If you understand this model and those you are relating to do not, and then you just happen to bring to their attention what they are doing in the bid for power stage, you will likely have a negative response or even an explosion.

Exposing what people are doing and giving it a negative name like "bid for power" is to court hurt feelings and perhaps hard feelings. More than likely, the others have never realized, or even thought about, how they relate or respond to others in a group.

At best, the relationships you are attempting to move forward will be set back; at worst, they could be destroyed. People just do not appreciate having their behavior analyzed and they do not appreciate being exposed as making a "bid for power" when that was the farthest thing from their conscious mind.

Most people go through these stages of interaction automatically and seldom give thought to the dynamics taking place.

Now, after this caution, we can take a detailed look at the model.

DETAILED ANALYSIS OF THE MODEL

POLITE STAGE: *In the first step, or the "polite stage," group members are getting acquainted, sharing values and establishing the basis for a group structure.* The group members are putting their best foot forward to establish, or project, as good an image as possible. As humans, we all need to be liked.

During this first stage, people are attempting to get to know one another and share information about themselves. This information will help them anticipate how others might respond later.

Personal agendas usually stay hidden during this first stage, but common associations with others of like mind are identified and future cliques have their birth in this stage. In groups where this polite stage is omitted, participants tend to be uncomfortable and have difficulty relating.

Why We Are Here Stage: *In the second stage, or the "Why are we here?" stage, someone will pose this question in one way or another and the group will move out of the polite stage and begin to define their purpose, their objectives and their goals.*

If the purpose for the group is socially oriented, little time will need to be spent in this second stage. However, if its purpose is task oriented, more time will need to be spent to find agreement of goals.

After bringing together a city-reaching group, the task would be to come corporately into the presence of the Lord and to seek His will for the city.

In this second phase, cliques, or to use a more sanitized phrase, "those with like minds," will most likely begin to form, and to exercise influence as the like-minded members find a common purpose. Hidden agendas begin to come out into the open as members try to exert influence toward objectives most satisfying to themselves.

Identity as a group is still low in this second phase but group members will begin to take risks as they display commitment to particular purposes or goals for the group. Leadership and group structure begins to emerge at this stage.

Some groups have a social purpose, such as men's groups, women's groups or couple's fellowship in the church, and they have little reason to leave the preceding polite stage. Some similar groups seem to agree not to grow, but simply relate in fellowship at the polite stage. They may agree to non-growth in order to keep from personally experiencing social deprivation in their lives, or it may be they simply desire to have a release valve for the other pressures in their lives.

However, once a diverse group comes together with a heart to reach out to their city, time must be spent in the "why we are hear" stage seeking the presence of the Lord and His leading for their purpose and goals. This leads to the third stage.

BID FOR POWER STAGE: *The third stage consists of the "bid for power." Again, a caution is needed here. Usually people do not consider what they do in a group as a bid for power. Rather, they believe they are advancing what they think is best for the group* —never considering that it may really be what is best for them; or they may be simply carrying out some preconceived notions they may have had.

This third stage will begin to be phased in as the group moves in the direction of considering purpose, goals and objectives. It may be seen when individuals within the group are attempting to influence other group members. They may be attempting to change the ideas, opinions and values of others, and never thinking about controlling behavior. Individuals may put forth their own ideas, opinions or values in opposition to, or counter to, what others have expressed. They may think the group should be doing something different from that of what others may have expressed and they voice their opinion about that.

This third stage is characterized by competition for influence, attention and recognition. In this phase some group members may try to rationalize their own positions and try to convince the group to take the action he or she feels is appropriate. Some members may even become closed-minded and not listen to others.

Tension, challenge or conflict within the group is higher in this stage than in any of the other stages. When two or more people believe they hear what the Lord is saying and it is different, something has to give. If the group has agreed to some simple guidelines for confirmation of a word from the Lord, the tension will be greatly reduced.

A struggle for leadership will likely occur in this stage, and that struggle may involve participation of all the subgroups within the core group.

Typical attempts to resolve any struggle for leadership usually involve seeking compromise, seeking a consensus, seeking a vote or seeking help from outside the group.

Hidden agenda items begin to surface and this causes behavioral change. Some, who were able to conceal their agenda in the earlier stages, find that other group members are becoming aware of it.

This is not to say that different ideas are not good. On the contrary, they are necessary and needed. However, what is required is cooperation and active listening, as well as an effort to combine ideas in a synergy that will lead to a stronger group idea. The only viable solution for a Christian group is to stay in the presence of the Lord until there is agreement on what the Lord is saying.

Some groups falter in their group growth at this phase. The group will not feel a strong team spirit and in fact, some members, who contributed freely in the first two phases, may no longer contribute.

Some members may feel very awkward if tension, hostility or competition begins to surface.

Some members may be tempted to throw up their hands in frustration and comment that they do not need this nor have the time for this; they may even withdraw from the group.

Some members will be frustrated because others in the group will not stop operating through their own flesh. It must be noted that not everyone in the group will stop operating from his or her own flesh at the same time.

Participation in the group in this phase can be very uncomfortable for some and this will cause the falter. Creative suggestions to move toward God's purpose may not be considered because of the perception of hidden agendas.

More will be discussed on the difficulty of this phase toward the end of the chapter.

Some groups never grow past this stage, especially if there is one or more highly competitive, strong willed or passive-aggressive individuals in the group.

Individual roles played by the different members in the group are especially important at this point if the group is to survive and be a positive contributor to the city-reaching endeavor.

The individual roles needing to be filled involve some group dynamic skills. However, the individuals filling these roles do not need to have special training in group dynamic skills. Many people simply develop these skills on their own by relating to other people.

The skill of *harmonizer* needs to help bring harmony. The skill of *compromiser* needs to help find a compromised solution to the power struggle. The skill of *gatekeeper* needs to help keep the door open to include all members. The skill of *follower* needs to help maintain an acceptable balance between the needs of the individual and the needs of the group.

Spiritually mature individuals in the group need to help keep the focus on giving glory to God, holiness, submission and obedience. *Aggressive* group members need to help press for group consensus.

If at least some of these group dynamic skills do not exist among the different members, the group may falter, and most likely not be able to move out of this bid for power stage and into the next.

Once the group has been able to overcome the difficulties of the third phase, it begins to be characterized by an attitude of change. Change takes place when some members give up their attempts to control and when they change their own attitude to that of active listening to others and focusing on God being in charge and leading the group.

Listening to each other and full submission to God are the key activities to overcoming the pitfalls of the bid for power phase.

CONSTRUCTIVE STAGE: ***The fourth phase is the "constructive stage." It is here group members are willing to change their preconceived ideas.*** That change may be based on submission to the Lord and based on facts presented by other members. A team spirit starts to build and cliques start to dissolve.

In the fourth phase, real progress starts to take place and leadership will have emerged. The group takes on its own identity and the members believe that identity is important. Leadership becomes a shared leadership.

When conflict arises, it is brought to the Lord and is dealt with by the whole group as a mutual problem.

The major difference between the constructive phase, or phase four, and the bid for power in phase three is the willingness of members to enter the presence of the Lord corporately, to listen to others, and to change based on what the other members say they are hearing from the Lord.

Because of this difference, the members in phase four will often use the talents and gifting of any of the members who are able to contribute. Creativity is often high in this phase because it is encouraged by the members; for this reason, group decisions are almost always better than any single member's input.

The leadership of a phase four constructive group is most effective when leading the group in seeking the Lord and ensuring everything is done to bring glory to the Lord.

The group leader is also most effective in phase four when asking constructive questions, clarifying and summarizing the group's thinking, trusting the group, blending in with the group, and not making any comments that would tend to reward or punish other group members.

The leadership of the phase four group will also recognize the different range of ability and maturity level within the group to contribute to any particular undertaking— and they will be tolerant of that variety.

UNITY AND COMMON PURPOSE STAGE: *The fifth and final phase of group growth is the "unity and common purpose" stage of group members or the esprit de corps stage.* This is a wonderful place to be and *it is what Jesus prayed for in John 17 in His high priestly prayer.* It is also a difficult place to get to and to maintain.

In this fifth phase, the group feels a high sense of unity with Christ and each other and a high sense of morale. Members are empathetic in their relationships and there is intense loyalty. The need for group approval is absent because each member approves of all the others in the group and accepts them as individuals.

In this phase, individuality is high and creativity is high. There is a sense that we may not always agree but we will respect other's opinions and we know they will respect ours. There is a freedom for the group member to express his or her individuality and cliques are absent.

Group identity becomes very important and the group may desire an identification symbol such as a logo for shirts, or a name card with their group identity. Camaraderie is very high, and there is a minimum need for structure—except for groups working on specific tasks.

There is a strong closeness of the group and it is impossible to bring in a new group member without destroying the group feeling and camaraderie.

When a new member does join the group, the group will need to go back to some previous stage in the process of the model.

Even though the group may go back to some previous stage, the steps may be easier to take and the process may move more rapidly. However, the third stage of the bid for power may again create an obstacle. Whether or not an obstacle is created will depend mostly on the personality, the spiritual maturity and the strength of will of the new member, as well as whether or not he or she makes a strong bid for power.

IMPORTANCE OF GROUP GROWTH TO CITY-REACHING

In any city-reaching endeavor there is going to have to be a core leadership team. That team needs to be aware of its role as a group and aware of how the enemy will try to divide and distract the group.

The stages of group growth must be given serious attention by the core leadership as they build toward unity of purpose and oneness—of *esprit de corps*. It is hoped that information about these five phases of group growth will assist in that effort.

It is of particular importance for those in the city-reaching movement to be aware that the third stage, the bid for power phase, is most crucial to the success of transforming the community. It is here that the enemy is most likely to enter in and sabotage the whole effort. It is also here that people will find out if they can work together on a voluntary basis.

CRITICALNESS OF THE BID FOR POWER STAGE

It is in the bid for power stage that Satan will pit one person against another, establish cliques or set up sides on an issue or approach. It is here that feelings get hurt and people experience inner discomfort, and sometimes, even pain.

The tendency of humans is to move away from pain and discomfort. When conflict and power struggles are experienced people tend to polarize, especially when they do not see the scheme of the enemy and what he is doing.

It is in the bid for power stage that those group members not directly involved in the power struggle will feel very uncomfortable and likely say, "I just do not need this." It is then that the core leadership team may begin to disintegrate. In like manner, those engaged in the bid for power, may well become more competitive, determined or combative. Possibly either, or both, parties will leave the group.

No matter which way it goes in the bid for power, there can be unspoken hurt and inner pain. This is the work of the enemy. This is why it is so important for the group to be aware of how the enemy will work. It is also extremely important for those who have group skills of human relations to use them. Members need to use their group skills of harmonizer, compromiser, gatekeeper, follower and the spiritually mature need to assert that maturity.

APPLICATION FOR CITY-REACHING

Think for a moment of the many past efforts at city-reaching. What has happened to them? Many have just disappeared over time. Who is going to talk about the hurt or the pain or the distrust or the uncooperativeness of others? *The efforts toward unity fall apart at the bid for power stage, if that stage does not get ad-equately resolved.* Out of a lack of commitment or lack of time, people will simply move away from situations that cause frustration, discomfort, pain, time wasting, inef-fectiveness and/or disappointment.

A major solution to the failure of city-reaching efforts is to deal with the issue of the stages of core leadership growth, especially the vulnerability of the bid for power stage; in doing that we will to be better prepared to ad-dress the schemes of the enemy, especially his attempts to divide.

When it comes to group growth, practical ways to defeat the enemy include the following: active listening between the competitive parties, assis-tance from the spiritually mature, diligent and honest prayer, courage to confront the issues, and group dynamic skills.

The sooner the hidden agendas are exposed and the issue of power gets resolved, the sooner the group can get on with kingdom business and get out of Satan's play-ground.

This issue of group growth is an issue that can-not be ignored. When we ignore the issue, we may soon be wondering what happened and how the project or vision just fell apart or faded away.

The issue of group growth takes place not only between members of the core leadership team, but between the team and other groups as they become involved in the city-reaching process. It also takes place between the differ-ent groups or churches that are, or become, involved. For example, as the core leadership team is formed, it goes through the five steps of group growth among itself. Then the core leadership team goes through the steps again along with the other groups (usually pastors for different churches). Then the pastors from the different churches go through the steps with each other.

The whole process is one of reaching unity in Christ, the unity that Christ prayed for in John 17. *We must be willing to embrace the discomfort, the hurt and the*

*pain and be willing to deal person-to-person with
other people. There is just no other way to develop
unity and become one in Christ.* There is no other way
to reach unity of purpose and join one transformed heart
with another until our community is transformed.

THE MCI MODEL

An example of a model we have for group growth is
seen at Marion Correctional Institution when the warden
and John Beason talked to the Aryan Brotherhood gang
in the chapel; SJ, one of the top lieutenants, turned his
back on John and crossed his arms indicating he would
not hear what was being said. When the Aryan Brotherhood members talked it over, calmer members helped SJ
to see the advantage of unity. Risks were taken on both
sides, the decision to go along with John's change for Christ
was made and the rest is history.

We must be willing to step out of our comfort zone and
risk dealing on a human level, person-to-person. We can
no longer run back to our comfortable life within the four
walls of the church, and just wait for Christ's prayer to be
answered to make us one. It is easy to deal with things
like systems, processes, procedures, techniques, policies,
buildings, etc. but it is not easy to deal with human relationships and the exchanges between people. We do well
at dealing with the natural world and even at joining to
pray against strongholds and demonic forces, but we falter terribly when it comes to developing unity and oneness. We need to learn about group growth so that we can
get on with advancing God's kingdom.

REPEAT CAUTION

Again, for the third time, the major caution needs to
be repeated; when confronted with the bid for power stage
in a group setting, do not use the term "power" in reference to what someone else is doing or saying.

The word "power" is a raw word and it will bring out
defensiveness in people. People do not think in terms of

power, or agendas, or one-up-man-ship when dealing with others. Rather they will tend to think in terms of "what they think is best," that they are "just expressing their opinion" or that "they are just trying to help" and they will communicate that message to the group in one way or the other. Their own self-interest usually remains hidden, even from themselves.

We will turn now to a consideration of the concepts of power and influence. These are concepts that are used by all people in their interactions with others, even though few people are able to verbalize it. Additionally, very few people would ever acknowledge they would, or do, use such a thing as power or influence.

James 4:7 (NLT)
So humble yourselves before God. Resist the Devil, and he will flee from you.

Matthew 12:25 (NLT)
Jesus knew their thoughts and replied, "Any kingdom at war with itself is doomed. A city or home divided against itself is doomed.

POWER AND INFLUENCE

INTRODUCTION

This chapter is the second part of the related topic of relationships and human interaction. It deals with understanding the different bases of power and influence and understanding how those bases are used in group relations, and between individuals. It is essential for those in leadership to grasp this concept of bases of power if they are going to adequately deal with the dynamics and relationships that take place between people in groups.

The different individuals and groups need to be encouraged, channeled, empowered and released to use their gifts and talents, as well as their creative and collaborative efforts in community transformation.

DEFINITIONS

So that we will be talking the same language, we will give some definitions of terms as they are used in this book.

By **power,** we mean the ability to influence others.

By **influence,** we mean the ability to motivate others to change their attitudes or behaviors.

By **motivate,** we mean the process that causes others to sustain or change a behavior because of some intrinsic or extrinsic source.

By **leadership,** we mean that which occurs when we motivate others to sustain a behavior or when we motivate others to change a behavior or an attitude.

By **empowerment,** we mean giving control of the decision-making process to those people affected and allowing them to have authority to match their responsibilities.

By **disempowerment,** we mean that those people who are affected do not have control of the decision-making process, they are dependent upon the leader or leadership team and they lack authority to fulfill their responsibilities.

By **bases of power or influence,** we mean that the bases of power and the bases of influence are the same.

Hidden Issues of the Heart

Research over the years has revealed nine different forms, or bases, of power or influence. These bases of power and influence will be discussed in detail under the section heading of Basis of Power and Influence.

People, as well as groups of people, use these bases of power and influence in their interactions with others. *In almost all interactions between people or between different groups, at least one of these forms of power or influence is at work.*

The different bases of power can be used to motivate people or groups; they can be, and are, used in the "bid for power" phase discussed in the last chapter dealing with group growth.

The way in which people use these bases of power and influence determines whether the atmosphere will be positive or negative, and it also determines the kind of climate or culture that is created. Please do not miss this point because it is extremely important in understanding relationship dynamics be-

tween people in all walks of life. These nine bases of power also give a framework for leaders to adjust their particular style of leadership in given situations. In using these bases of power the leader of a group can either empower or disempower other members of the group.

Again, this issue of power and influence is an issue that is not openly dealt with in groups, and especially in those groups desiring community transformation. Rather, it is usually a hidden issue and sometimes it is even a subconscious or unrecognized issue within groups, especially those groups desiring to do the will of God.

Somehow, using power and influence to achieve a goal just does not seem like the godly thing to be doing. It somehow seems like one is exerting undue pressure on another individual to get what one wants. It seems like one is trying to control another, and that is openly unacceptable in our independent American culture. As a result, the topic is usually not discussed.

Yet, power and influence are subtly used in almost every relationship. Our sensitive feelings about the use of power come from a lack of understanding of the nature of power and influence; it can be used for good as well as for bad. We need to learn the difference and use it for the good.

It is important for us to learn something about the bases of power and influence if we are to understand the dynamics of how we are going to come into unity to influence our cities for Christ.

Empowerment by Core Leadership

Often times the term "empowered" is used as a "buzzword" when people are not truly empowered. The city-reaching effort must truly empower different groups by allowing the groups to be able to empower themselves.

The many different streams of churches, ministries, groups, people, organizations, as well as institutions of government, religion, business, economic and education are all required to influence community change. *They must not feel they will lose any autonomy, but rather that they may empower themselves to participate at the level that is appropriate for them at any particular time.*

The leadership of the citywide movement must release and encourage the different streams to empower themselves and to become involved according to their own timing. As the presence of Christ increases in the city, those different streams will gradually become more and more involved.

We have to remember that a city will become transformed starting with one person worshiping and being in the presence of God. That one person brings God's kingdom to the city in his or her own sphere of influence. Then, one by one, group by group, God's presence will begin to fill the city and begin to be recognized.

This statement is so simple and yet we do not see it happening in America. However, this is what has happened at Marion Correctional Institution and that is why we need to be aware of how we increase God's kingdom person by person.

The key role of the core leadership team in the city transformation effort is that of networking and establishing connections and relationships between the vast numbers of streams that are needed to change the city. Their role should be to connect the different needs in the city with different streams that are empowered, through a legitimate movement, to meet those needs.

BASIS OF POWER AND INFLUENCE

The original typology of power was developed by French and Raven[1] and it included five bases of power. Those bases of power were *expert, referent* (personality), *position, reward* and *coercion.* Later, Raven and Kruglanski[2] described *information* power. *Connection* power was added by Hersey and Goldsmith[3]. Sergiovanni and Starratt[4] added *moral* power to the research on power and influence. C. Bulach[5] then added *ego* power to the research literature.

I will first list the bases of power and influence and then discuss each in turn. *The first five listed below usually have positive affects on people* in that they can be used to empower people. *The last four can affect people in a negative way* because they usually, though not always, are used for controlling people.

The bases of power or influence are as follows: 1) Information; 2) Expertise; 3) Personality; 4) Ego; 5) Moral; 6) Position; 7) Reward; 8) Coercion; and 9) Connection. Remember, the first five usually have a positive impact on people and the last four usually have a negative impact.

Information power. *This is when one person has access to information that may be needed or may be helpful to others.* Some have claimed that knowledge is power; however, knowledge is information and information is power.

The information can be used by the individual group member or by the entire core leadership group for positive or for negative purposes. If the information is used to enhance others it definitely is a positive. However, if it is used to give selected individuals or groups an edge or advantage, it will eventually be viewed as negative. In that case, the unity that the core leadership is trying to develop will be in danger of a breakdown.

Expert power. *This applies when the individual group member or the whole group is perceived by those who can be influenced, as having superior knowledge or ability in given areas.*

When the need arises, this base of power can be used to help another person or group. When expert power is solicited and given, it is perceived as positive

However, when expert power is unsolicited, it can be viewed as an unwanted intrusion and is therefore seen as negative.

Expert power by itself is a very limited power base. Its continual use can put up barriers between the user and others, and those barriers can be difficult to remove. The way in which the expertise is delivered has a lot to do with whether it is perceived as positive or negative.

It is important for the core leadership team to monitor the use of experts and be sure that a large portion of humility goes with its use. If the person or group using the expert power base is in any way condescending or authoritative in manner it will most likely be seen as a putdown. Likewise, that person or group who puff themselves up or overuse the words "I," "me," or "us" show their own insecurities and quickly become overbearing.

PERSONALITY POWER. *Even though this base of power is informal, this person's, or group's, peers and colleagues respect them and want their approval. Those who have this form of power use it frequently.*

Personality power is an identification process; there is a bond created between those who have this base of power and those who are influenced by it. The bond that exists is created by a sense of common purpose, of common beliefs, of common views and of common interests. In addition, the sheer magnetism or charisma held by the person or group who possesses this base of power creates a bond with those influenced by it.

It is possible to have a sense of common purpose, beliefs, views and interests without the charisma of some person or group; however, when combined with personality power the commonality is particularly strong.

For the core leadership team it is important to monitor the use of the personality power base, either by themselves or by others, because overuse of this base of power can cause other individuals or group members to begin to grumble and feel taken advantage of.

For the most part the personality power base is seen as very positive. It is not something that can be developed like learning to become an expert or like getting promoted to a higher position. Either a person or a group has it or they do not. Everyone has some charisma and no one has perfect charisma.

To the extent that the core leadership has this basis of power, or is able to identify it in others, it should be used—but not overused.

EGO POWER. *This power is gained by knowing whose ego to stroke and when to stroke that ego.*

Stroking others can be considered as manipulative when overdone and group members will perceive that they are being used. Also, stroking too many people often, and in the presence of others, may be viewed as insincere and can have a negative affect.

MORAL POWER. *Moral power is getting others to change their behavior based on commonly held moral beliefs or convictions.*

Attempting to use moral power is a mistake when there is not agreement on the expectations, values, and ideas that are to govern behavior. If agreement does not exist, the person using moral power will likely be viewed as trying to impose his or her own set of values on the others. This may well cause the individual or group to get the reputation of being self-righteous.

The group must have common understandings and agreement on foundational principles as well as on expectations that are going to be followed. This is especially important as the core leadership group begins to reach out to encourage other streams to join in efforts of collaboration.

If the core leadership were to come along after the fact and try to enforce or change behavior or beliefs based on moral convictions, it would more than likely get the core leadership group labeled as judgmental or fanatical.

LEGITIMATE OR POSITION POWER. *Legitimate power is defined as a person or group holding a particular position of leadership or authority.* For example, a person may hold the position of chairperson of a committee; he may not have any other power, but based on his position as chairperson, he has legitimate power. The official leader of any organization holds legitimate power by virtue of that position.

It is important that any movement to facilitate and coordinate the city-reaching efforts be given legitimate status and fall under authority of recognized city elders from across denominational lines.

If you have legitimate power you will find others willing to follow you due to the importance given to the legitimate role played by the core leadership team in the city-reaching effort.

Serious power struggles have occurred between different groups attempting to establish themselves as the legitimate authority for city-reaching endeavors. For example, there have been lone rangers attempting to pull together their own group with themselves as the overseeing apostle.

Power struggles, like cliques, are designed by the enemy to divide and destroy any community transformation efforts. They must be dealt with and this takes courage from the core leadership team; it may mean being willing to embrace discomfort or conflict that we would much rather not have to deal with.

Reward power. *When an individual or core leadership group gives a positive stroke, some form of remuneration, award or any symbolic gesture that is seen as a compliment, they are exercising reward power.*

It is important to remember that the core leadership team in a city-reaching endeavor acts as a project director coordinating, encouraging, facilitating and channeling the efforts of many unrelated and autonomous streams in the community. Using its legitimate position as a platform for using its reward power is essential.

Failure to reward those groups that deserve reward can create concerns about lack of appreciation on that group's part and may hinder further cooperation or participation.

If the core leadership group shows any favoritism, it is a misuse of reward power. Another mistake is to over-use reward power to the point where reward loses meaning.

Over use of reward power can create a, "what's in it for me?" mentality where some of the different streams may not participate unless they know they will be rewarded, or get what they want out of their cooperation.

Coercive power. *This applies to the ability of one person or group to punish the person or group being influenced in some way.* This may involve material punishment such as removal from committees or position as well as personal punishment such as potential disapproval, rejection or dislike[6]. It may also simply be withholding reward.

Coercive behaviors are verbal or non-verbal put-downs, slights, or pressure to force a behavior. A demotion, an unwanted transfer or the withholding of some needed resource are even more extreme forms of coercive power.

Leaders who quickly resort to coercion as a way to induce follower compliance will soon lose their position of influence because members will not take the abuse for long. They may rebel or undermine the leader, or they may just leave; this is especially true when group members have a choice in participating, such as in volunteer groups.

CONNECTION POWER. *This form of power is described by how group members perceive that their leader has connecting associations with other influential people.*

If group members perceive their leader is well connected with influential persons of higher status or position, their own position power is enhanced. The group members know that their leader has greater ability to reward, punish or receive status for them than someone who is not so well connected. When this base of power is combined with position power, it gives the leader even greater power to influence and increases the likelihood of compliance.

This base of power is gained for the leader by how the members perceive his or her connections with other influential people. If members perceive the leader has connection, then that leader has the power, even though in reality he or she may not have the connection. The group member will comply with the leader based on that member's belief that the leader has the connection.

One misuse of connection power is when a leader "drops names" to enhance his or her own status or power and influence. Another misuse is the leader who tries to force compliance by name-dropping statements like: "I'm going to talk to (the connection)."

SUMMARY OF BASES OF POWER

The nine bases of power and influence can be used for good or for bad purposes. They are used not only by group leaders but by group members as well, but make no mistake about it, used they are!

It was mentioned that power and influence are at the foundation of all relationships. Therefore, it is information of which those persons actively involved in city transformation must be aware.

There needs to be an intentional effort to use these bases of power and influence in a positive and constructive manner to empower people and to move people to higher levels of maturity in the Lord in what they are doing. A special effort must be made not to use the bases of power in a negative way to control people and to enhance self.

Ask any marriage counselor and he will tell you that at the root of almost any marriage problem, lays the issue of power. As we forge the necessary relationships with the many different streams required to change our city we must learn to work effectively with those streams using the positive aspects of the bases of power and influence.

The basic root of most, if not all, relationship problems is based on the power to control another, and that root is mostly driven by pride. It is amazing that the issue stays so hidden and that it is so well covered up by people.

One effort of this book is to identify some of those hidden issues that are at the heart of much of our lack of success in transforming our cities. For many of these issues it is simply not acceptable to discuss openly in America, especially if we ourselves may somehow be involved.

Power and influence are realities to be dealt with. They are persuasive, potent and effective tools when used properly and they need to be mastered by those desiring city transformation. The tools can also be very destructive when used improperly to enhance self or gain some advantage.

PART 4
CONCLUSION

Introduction to Part 4

The state of the church is a sobering message to all ministers, and this does not mean just pulpit pastors; it is a message to all of us because we are all ministers.

Chapter 12 lays out a summary of where we have been and where we have come to in our travel through this book.

Chapter 13 provides some possible next steps for us if we desire to see our own lives, as well as our individual churches and our cities, transformed.

1 John 2:15-17 (NLT)

Stop loving this evil world and all that it offers you, for when you love the world, you show that you do not have the love of the Father in you. ¹⁶For the world offers only the lust for physical pleasure, the lust for everything we see, and pride in our possessions. These are not from the Father. They are from this evil world. ¹⁷And this world is fading away, along with everything it craves. But if you do the will of God, you will live forever.

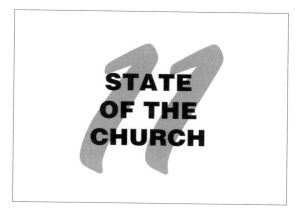

BACKGROUND

In the Book of Revelation, Jesus Christ gave us His message to the churches down through the ages. This is Christ's message to us and we dare not ignore it. It is a message He wants us to know and it is a message He meant for us to understand.

It is easy today for many to criticize and to complain about the church. Since it is a season of decadence in the world, it is easy to blame the church for not making a difference in our troubled and evil world. However, Christ says in the book of Revelation that the endtimes will be evil, but there will also be a tremendous harvest of souls. That tremendous harvest of souls is happening today. People around the world are coming to the Lord in record numbers

The message of Christ to the churches in Revelation is a message of hope. It is my intent in this book to carry that message of hope to the churches so the broken walls can be rebuilt. *We need to reignite and reawaken the workers in the many different churches to carry Christ's message of hope to the lost souls who so desperately need Him.*

We will only consider here what it is Jesus says to the churches; His message is covered in chapters two and three of the book of Revelation. In these chapters, Jesus gives us understanding into the different types of churches, as they existed when He gave the message, as they existed down through the ages and as they exist today. Since our topic is the state of the church, there is no better place to receive an understanding of the church than from Jesus Himself.

There are four major interpretations of the book of Revelation but the weaknesses outweigh the strengths in three of them. Without getting into a discussion on interpretation, suffice it to say here that *the position taken in this book is that each church represents a particular type of church throughout the church age.* Some interpreters go so far as to say that each church represents a particular church age and that we are in the church age of the church of Laodicea. That may be so, but I believe there is a better argument that each church mentioned is representative of churches throughout each age.

In other words, even though today many churches may have the characteristics of the church of Laodicea, there are also in existence churches with the characteristics of each of the other types of churches identified by Christ.

We need to understand that there were additional churches in existence in Asia, besides the seven mentioned by Christ at the time He gave this revelation to John. It is believed the other churches were not included with the seven because the seven churches discussed by Christ are characteristic of all churches that have existed through all ages, including today.

APPROACH TO THE TOPIC

We will now turn to a brief discussion of the seven churches and the discussion will cover the common topics

Jesus mentioned when He spoke about each of the different types of churches.

We will look first at the good things Jesus says about each, or His commendation.

Second, we will also look at what He has against each church, or His warning to the church.

Third, we will look at the counsel He has for the church.

Lastly, we will look at the promise He has for the church.

For each of the above topics, which Christ spoke to the church, there will be some descriptive application mentioned where appropriate.

Information for the descriptions and comments has been gleaned mostly from historical background of each of the original seven churches.

The material in this chapter is presented as a guide to help organize our thinking about churches today. A much more in-depth study is recommended for a full understanding of what Christ is saying to us today.

It must be remembered that in giving the first part of His message to the seven churches in Revelation 1:13, Christ is standing in the midst of the seven candlesticks, which are the seven churches themselves. This symbolizes Christ as the light of the world, and it is the task of each type of church to proclaim the light of Christ to the world. Each church receives its light from Christ and if He is not in its midst, the church has no light.

Christ's message to the churches is the Word of God, the Holy Scriptures, and that is the message the church is to proclaim.

We also need to remember that Christ tells us in Revelation 1:20 that the seven stars He holds in His right hand are the angels of the seven churches. The word angel in the Greek has two meanings; first, it means angel, or angelic being. Second, it means messenger.

Messengers are carriers of the Word; this includes pastors, but it means more than just pastors. It also means all those who minister God's Word—all those who comfort and minister to the needs of hurting

and needy people. It means all His ambassadors, or ministers, in the church today.

As Christ is speaking to the churches, He is holding the ministers in His right hand. This means Christ is directing His message to all ministers of all the types of churches down through the ages, as well as today. *Therefore, this is an awesome message for all those who are Christ's messengers—His ambassadors, or ministers in the church today.* His message to us is meant by Christ to be understood. What a responsibility on all who call themselves Christ's ambassadors!

CHURCH OF EPHESUS

Christ's commendations given to the ministers: The church works hard and it is patient and steadfast in its laboring for Christ. It does not tolerate sin or evil among its members and it tests and rejects false teaching and false apostles. It has suffered for the Lord and has not given up.

Christ's complaint given to the ministers: The church has lost its first love for Christ. It has focused so much on the labor, and on being doctrinally sound, that it has lost its focus on Christ. They are not fellowshipping with Christ the way they used to, and they are no longer walking in an awareness of His presence. They have become consumed with, and interested in, protecting themselves from the world—so much so, that they no longer have the time to spend in the presence of Christ. They no longer love Jesus Christ as they had before.

Christ's counsel given to the ministers: Repent and turn back to Him. Anytime a church or an individual turns away from Christ, the call from Christ is the same— repent and return.

Three things are involved in their returning. First, they are to remember where they came from.

Second, they are to repent. They are to turn away from whatever has pulled them away from Christ, those things that are consuming their minds and thoughts and keeping them from focusing their attention on Christ.

Third, they are to return to Christ and do the work that they had done before losing their focus on Him. They are to focus on Him and fellowship with Him; they are to get alone with Him and to acknowledge Him in everything they do.

Christ's warning given to the ministers: The warning Christ gives to this church has two parts.

First, they are warned that unless they return to Christ, He will remove the church (candlestick) from its place. What is the place of this church?

Its place is that of being the true church, the true representative of Christ on earth. Its place is being the light and witness of the gospel to the world.

Think for a moment of how many churches are dull and lifeless and lack the presence of Christ. This is a frightening warning.

Second, they are warned that having pure doctrine is just not enough. Christ says it is good that they hate the Nicolaitans who teach false doctrine but even though it is good, it is not enough. We know this because it falls under what Christ is giving as a warning to the church. The church had taught and warned against the false teaching of the Nicolaitans. They had refused to allow error into the church and they stood firmly for truth. Yet Christ says it is not enough; it is good, but it is not enough because it has distracted them from His presence.

So many of our churches today will argue and fight over doctrine and become so consumed with labeling as heresy those things that have nothing to do with the absolutes of the truth of Jesus Christ.

Christ's promise to the overcomers: The hope that Jesus gives to the overcomers is the promise of eating from the tree of life and being a citizen in God's paradise.

The idea of the word overcomer is that of conflict and struggle. The overcomer gains victory and we are to overcome everything that attempts to draw us away from Christ. We are to overcome those things that attract our heart and love away from Christ. ***All the lust of the flesh, the lust of the eyes and the pride of life continually*** *comes from the world to get our attention and steal our heart from Christ.* As long as we are in this world, we will face the conflict and struggle with the world, with our own desires and with Satan—but we are to be overcomers of all these things.

It is important to note that the promises of Christ are given only to the overcomers.

Church of Smyrna

Christ's commendations given to the ministers: Christ commended the church for four things. First, the church is standing up under terrible tribulation; there are pressures, affliction, trials and persecutions. They are refusing to denounce or deny Christ even in the face of martyrdom.

Second, the church is standing up under poverty, under having nothing and being destitute and still remaining faithful to Christ.

Third, the church is spiritually wealthy. It is inwardly rich in faithfulness, righteousness and holiness.

Lastly, the church is standing up under all kinds of slander. It is the slanderers who ridicule, mock, lie, backbite, criticize, spread rumors, make fun of, tear down and do all sorts of evil to destroy the church.

Christ says the slanderers are from the synagogue of Satan. This means they are people who profess being Christian, but they are not. They are from the religious church. *Just as it was the religious people who killed Jesus, we can expect the religious people of our day to persecute us.*

Christ's complaint given to the ministers: None. This is one of the few churches to whom Christ does not give a warning. The church stands faithful to Christ and to His mission and it stands fast against all attacks.

Christ's counsel given to the ministers: Christ lets the church know that the devil is going to bring more persecution for a short (ten days) period of time so the church will draw even closer to Him and have their faith strengthened even more.

When unbelievers see the church standing strong under severe persecution, it will cause some unbelievers to turn to Christ. That is the reason Christ is allowing the persecution and He counsels them not to fear, but to remain faithful.

How many of us are willing to suffer persecution so that our suffering would be a testimony to unbelievers? This is a very special church.

Christ's promise to the overcomers: There are two promises given. First, they will receive a crown of life, which is the reward of eternal life.

Second, they shall be delivered from the second death. Scripture clearly tells us that the second death is the lake of fire, the judgment of eternal hell, torment and separation from God for eternity.

We should know with certainty that there is a second death, but that we can escape it by being faithful to Christ. Faithful even when it means persecutions, sufferings and even experiencing the first death here on earth.

The fluff that is taught in some churches today, that life as a Christian is peaches and cream, is very misleading. The peaches and cream part is on the inside of us, in our inner relationship with Christ; it is not peaches and cream on the outside of us—in the world. We live in an evil and sinful world. *Therefore, according to Christ, we should expect more and more persecution, pain and suffering the closer we get to the time of His return. However, that persecution will be for the purpose of our being a testimony to unbelievers and it will turn some of them to Christ.*

CHURCH OF PERGAMOS

Christ's commendations given to the ministers: Christ has three commendations for the church. First, it has remained loyal to Christ's name. The church is located in the midst of worldliness, it is located in the midst of Satan's kingdom and they still would not deny Christ.

They could have lived in obscurity and secretly worshiped Christ, but they did not do that. They wanted their loved ones and their neighbors to know about Christ. They gave their testimony and refused to deny Christ.

Second, they did not water down the truth or soften their doctrine of Christ. They maintained their faith in Christ, they preached about Christ and they studied the Word of Christ.

Lastly, they stood fast in the face of persecution, even when one of their own members was martyred. The Greek word for martyr is witness. We are all called, like this church, to be witnesses, which means we are called to be martyrs.

Christ's complaint given to the ministers: They were guilty of the false doctrine of Balaam and of worldliness. It was a worldly church even if it remained faithful to the name of Christ, even if it preached and taught that Christ was the Son of God and came to earth to pay for our sins.

The corruption and worldliness surrounding the church had infiltrated into the church itself. They had a mixture of religion and of worldliness. They baptized people who had never repented. They allowed the worldly people to teach. They had mixed membership of believers and unbelievers who ran the church and determined its policies.

The results of allowing unbelievers to govern and to teach a diluted gospel are tragic for any church and leads to immorality, addictions and witchcraft within the church. *There are many tragic churches of Pergamos today. This is one reason why it is so difficult today to tell the difference between churchgoers and nonbelievers in the world.*

It needs to be noted that for those churches that received commendations from Christ, there had to be some people in that church who were still standing firm.

Christ's counsel given to the ministers: Repent. The church and its believers were to repent and deal with the unbelievers who were worldly, and they needed to change old practices of unbelievers holding positions of authority in the church. They needed to have evidence of repentance and acceptance of the Lord by the unbelievers, and they needed to stop baptizing unbelievers and giving them a sense of false hope.

Christ's warning given to the ministers: Christ warns that He will come quickly and make war against the unbelievers, against those who refuse to repent of their worldliness.

Christ will punish those who refuse to repent. However, He will not punish those who do repent and believe the gospel, those who turn away from the world in repentance.

Christ's promise to the overcomers: There are two promises given. First, they will be able to eat the manna from heaven. This means Christ Himself; the overcomers will be able to feed spiritually on Christ who gives life to man. Therefore, the person who stops feeding from the world will be given Christ for spiritual nourishment.

Second, the overcomer will be given a white stone with a new name written on it. It is not clear what this means because the Bible does not say. It may mean that the stone is the believer's ticket into heaven.

Church of Thyatira

Christ's commendations given to the ministers: It is an active church with all kinds of work for the Lord. There are works of love and service, so their ministries showed love and care, interest and concern, all for the lost.

There are works of enduring and patient faith. Through its outreach with so many different ministries, there is growth in the church along with energy and activity.

Christ's complaint given to the ministers: The church has allowed Jezebel, who is a false prophet (male or female), to teach in the church. This means the church has compromised its standards of pure doctrine and of being in the world but not of the world.

Jezebel teaches false doctrine and teaches fornication and idolatry. This false prophet uses reasonable arguments to deceive and mislead people. Idolatry is having an idol in one's life. An idol is anything that is put before God and that consumes the person's mind and takes priority in the person's life. It could be money, work, position, possessions, sports, pleasure, sex, self, and the list could go on.

The arguments of a Jezebel have strong appeal to the people because the people are told what they want to hear and given permission to do what they want to do. The people are taught, in one way or the other, that they do not need to separate themselves from the world. It takes a strong pastor to confront and deal with a Jezebel in the church.

Christ's warning given to the ministers: The church is given several warnings by Christ. First, there is a warning to Jezebel that she is to be cast on a bed of sickness. This most likely means some form of venereal disease because her judgment will match her sin. She was given an opportunity to repent, but she did not.

Second, there is a warning given to Jezebel's followers; they will suffer the same judgment if they refuse to repent and turn to Christ. Even if they are not totally sold out to all of her teaching but only follow some of it, they will still receive her judgment. They are to repent of their sins of having anything to do with Jezebel.

Lastly, there is the warning to the children of Jezebel that the Lord would kill them with death. It is not clear what this means. It could mean her real children, but more likely means those who have believed and followed her false teaching, those who have sold out completely to her.

The reason Christ is going to judge those who compromise themselves with Jezebel is so that the world will know He is Lord over the universe, that He is the one who searches the minds and hearts of people. He will judge those who compromise so that judgment will be executed fairly.

Christ's counsel given to the ministers: They are to hold fast. Those who compromise with the world and refuse to live holy lives, live in sin. Christ is letting us know that He will not place burdens and demands upon us that we cannot bear, but we are not to have anything to do with those things that harm us.

Christ's promises to overcomers: To those who over-come the compromises with the world and the influence of Jezebel are first promised authority and power over nations.

The second promise given is the morning star. This is Jesus Christ Himself. The overcomer is never to be away from Christ.

What the Spirit is saying to this church is to never compromise and become corrupt with the sins of the world, to separate from the sins of the world and to never allow a Jezebel or any corrupt and compromising person to teach in the church.

Pastor, you need to lead the charge and deal with these people in your church. You will be held accountable to God for what you do about them. You must do what has to be done in God's strength. It is far better to lose your job from a compromising church than to be put out of heaven and eternal life with Christ.

CHURCH OF SARDIS

Christ's commendation given to the ministers: There is no commendation given to this church. None! That means that its sin is the most serious a church can have.

Christ's complaint given to the ministers: The pastor and the people appeared to be alive, but they were dead. To understand what this complaint is about we looked at the historical account of the church of Sardis.

Christ's complaint was based on the church having all kinds of ministry and activity and work going on. It had a very good reputation among the other churches; it had the right beliefs and doctrine but it was void of the Holy Spirit. The talents and gifts of people are what moved the church forward and not the Holy Spirit.

Churches of the Sardis type today focus on what man and money can do and not on what faith in Christ can do. They give lip service to having faith and point to all their activity and work as evidence of the faith they have and of what they call the blessings of the Lord; nonetheless they are spiritually dead. They have upbeat, emotional worship service time, but it is based on man's talents and performance. They use the buzzword today of being "seeker friendly" and they are careful not to offend anyone based on the rationale of not wanting to drive any nonbeliever away. Their altar calls, if they have them, are designed to be non-threatening (and noncommittal) with everyone's eyes closed and with everyone repeating the same prayer aloud at the same time after the pastor. The pastor then depends upon anyone praying the prayer for the first time to tell "someone."

Anyone would have a very difficult time telling this church that it was dead and lifeless. It has much human energy and human excitement, but it is void of the spiritual energy of the Holy Spirit. However, *their activities and human energy just do not have the Spirit of God in them and His power is not seen in the church. What is seen is what can be done by any gifted and talented group of people focused on their own vision for growth and success.* They are doing many of the things a church is supposed to be doing, but they are doing it without Christ.

Christ does acknowledge there are a few things in the church that still has some life left in them; however, those things are also in the process of dying.

Christ's counsel given to the ministers: The church is to watch. It is to wake up and become alert. It is to watch for those people or activities that show a glimpse of having the Spirit of Christ in them; it is to be alert to find them.

Then, the church is to strengthen those areas that have a glimmer of life left in them. It is to divert resources to them. It is to acknowledge and give support from the pulpit to those areas. It is to begin to focus on their spiritual strength. The pastor needs to acknowledge from the pulpit that they are dying and that change is required in motives and attitudes.

Christ's warning given to the ministers: Christ warns the dead church to do four things. First, they are to jog their memories and remember how they received the gospel. They must go back to the beginning and recall what it was like when they were doing their devotions and Bible studies. Recall how they were hungry for the Word when they first became a Christian. Recall how they were eager to witness, to serve and to do ministry.

Second, they were to stir up and arouse the spirit they first had in their early years as a Christian.

Third, they were to repent. They have lost their fervor and zeal for Christ by letting their own selves become satisfied and complacent.

Lastly, they must know that the judgment of Christ will be on them if they do not repent. Christ will strip them of all that they have and will come upon them as a thief in the night, unexpectedly and without warning; they must repent.

Christ's promises to the overcomers: A few people in the church have continued to stay Christ-focused and have not become involved in the activities and programs that enhanced the worldliness of the church. To these who are undefiled, Christ promises they will walk with the Lord in white.

Walking with the Lord in white means, the faithful believer will walk day by day in the presence of Christ and He will look after them keeping them pure (white).

There are three promises made to the overcomer. First, the overcomer will be clothed in white, in the righteousness and purity of Christ when he enters heaven.

Second, being blotted out of the book of life will not happen to the overcomer. Rather, the overcomer will receive eternal life.

Third, before God, Jesus Christ will acknowledge the overcomer.

Church of Philadelphia
Christ's commendations given to the ministers:

The church of Philadelphia is a picture of what a church should be. This is a church that is faithful to Christ and that is alive. Christ commends this church for three things. First, it is using the open door to evangelism and missions outreach that Christ has given them.

Second, they are faithful to God's Word and they keep His Word by studying it, living it and declaring it to others.

Third, they do not deny God's Word. They live, move and have their entire being in God. *Christ is the focus of all their programs, activities and worship. They do not cave in to the world as the world tries to lead them away from their focus on Christ.*

Christ's hope given to the ministers: Christ gives two hopes to hang on to for those churches that are represented by the church of Philadelphia. First, they will be vindicated before all their prosecutors. The prosecutors are those who claim to be believers but are not; they are liars and most do not even realize it.

Second, because the church has patiently obeyed Christ in spite of persecutions, Christ says He will deliver them from the great tribulation and from temptation. The hope is that Christ is going to deliver the faithful and alive church

Christ's counsel given to the ministers: This church must hold fast to what it has been doing and not let the world steal their devotion to winning souls. They must hold fast to the Word of Christ and hold fast to living for Christ. This church could lose its crown if it does not hold fast.

Christ's promises to the overcomers: Christ gives five promises to those believers and churches that hold fast to witnessing for Christ in their evangelism and missionary zeal; that hold fast by staying in the Word of Christ and staying true to the Word of Christ; that hold fast by confessing and living for Christ, never denying Him.

First, they will be made a pillar in the temple of God, meaning they will become a permanent and vital part of God's house.

Second, they will receive security, and never have to

go in or out of a place for security and they will be free from a corrupt world.

Third, they will receive God's name, which is a symbol of belonging to God, and of being His possession.

Fourth, they will receive the name of the new city, the New Jerusalem, meaning they will become citizens of the new capital city of heaven.

Last, they will receive Christ's new name; He has not yet revealed what that name is.

CHURCH OF LAODICEA

Christ's commendation given to the ministers: None! Christ does not commend the church of Laodicea for anything. He has nothing good to say about this church.

Christ's complaint given to the ministers: The church and its members are only lukewarm; they are neither hot nor cold. *This means they were only half-committed, complacent, lethargic, half-hearted, indifferent, and self-satisfied.*

This describes so many church members today, and their lukewarmness affects their commitment. They are only partially, if at all, committed to Christ and to proclaiming Him as the Son of God. They are only partially, if at all, committed to the Word of God, to evangelism, to missions, to witnessing, to Bible study, to supporting the church and to holy and pure living.

The list could go on and on, but it is frightening because the warning is so terrible and Christ directs the warning, through the ministers, to so many in the church today.

Christ's warning given to the ministers: Jesus Christ says to the self-satisfied, half-committed lukewarm church members today that He will spew them out of His mouth. *People today who claim to be Christian and a part of His Body, but who are lukewarm, are unappetizing food to the Body and unwanted by Christ in their lukewarm state. He will—not maybe, but will—spew them out.* He does not find the lukewarm food to be the kind of nourishment He wants for the Body.

Christ finds the lukewarm commitment of Christians nauseating. He will not give their nourishment to the Body, which is why He will spew them all out.

Christ rejects the lukewarm church and people for two reasons. First, the church felt it was rich and prosperous and in need of nothing. *The people believe their wealth and prosperity are the same as spirituality; they confuse material blessings with spiritual blessings. They think the Lord is blessing them with what they have and conclude they are all right with Him. As a result, the church and people have become independent, self-sufficient, self-centered and prideful.*

The church and the people focus on their own capabilities rather than on their need for Christ. Their church activities are a matter of form, of just doing church, instead of being in Christ. Their hunger and thirst after God is gone. They no longer have a true burden for the lost, and there is much self-sufficiency.

There are talented, energetic, professional church members and pastors who are quite capable. However, what they do is done in the flesh, and not in the Spirit of God.

The second reason Christ rejects them is because of who they truly are on the inside; they are wretched, miserable, poor, blind and naked. All these things mentioned by Christ refer to the spiritual condition of the people.

Being wretched on the inside means to be afflicted spiritually, to be contemptible and inferior. In God's eyes, they are spiritually lacking.

Being miserable on the inside means to be pitied and despicable. They are doing things in their own strength. They are missing being in Christ and doing His work in His power, so they are to be pitied.

Being poor on the inside means that even though they have worldly riches on the outside, they have no spiritual riches on the inside.

Being blind on the inside means they cannot see the spiritual need inside themselves or inside others. They cannot see the possibilities of the spiritual, supernatural power of the Holy Spirit working in the human soul and in the church.

Being naked on the inside means they do not see the need for being clothed by the righteousness of Christ because they are not even aware they are naked on the inside. They believe they are good enough because they do good things and are good people. They do very little thinking about their need for righteousness and holiness, because that is what being a good person means to them. They give little or no thought to why it was necessary for Christ to die for their sins and the sins of the world.

Christ's counsel given to the ministers: Christ counsels the church to do three things. First, they are to buy spiritual gold, spiritual clothing and spiritual eye salve.

Buying spiritual gold means spiritual wealth, so the church can be truly wealthy. Spiritual wealth is the fruit of the Spirit of love, joy, peace, patience, goodness, kindness, faithfulness, gentleness and self-control; it is also confidence, security and hope. Material wealth cannot give the things that keep a person healthy, or that ease loneliness and emptiness or that satisfy the soul. Spiritual wealth, on the other hand, is found only in Christ.

Buying spiritual clothing means that no matter how much physical clothing they have, they lack the real spiritual clothing to cover their spiritual nakedness. The spiritual clothing is the righteousness of Christ and they need to be spiritually clothed in His righteousness

We are only accepted by God because we have on the righteousness of Christ. God does not accept us because we are members of a church, been baptized, are good people, do good things, believe there is a God or that Christ is His Son (even the demons believe this). There is only one way we are acceptable to God and that is to be clothed in the righteousness of Christ. If we are not in Christ, we will appear before God in our own righteousness and we will be naked and ashamed.

Buying spiritual eye salve means that no matter how

much we buy material eye salve to treat our eyes so we can see the things of God, we will continue to remain blind to what He is doing, and we will still be in the spiritual darkness.

We will not see the spiritual light of the world, which is Jesus Christ. We will only see our own worldly and prosperous life, our own good works, our own abilities and talents and our own wisdom and gifts. We will not see what the presence and power of Christ can do for our church and for us. Spiritual eye salve will help us see spiritual truth.

The second counsel Christ gives the church is to be zealous and repent. Even though we are only lukewarm and half-committed, Christ still loves us with a tender, brotherly love. It is not His anger that is rebuking us; it is His love for us.

Our behavior is so wrong that Christ exhorts us to be zealous in our repenting. A half-hearted, half-committed repentance will never do. What is required is a sobbing, weeping, heart wrenching repentance by us; we need to boil and burn with zeal, sincerity and earnestness in our turning from our Laodicea lifestyle.

Lastly, Christ counsels the church to open the door of our hearts for Him to come in.

He is standing at our heart's door showing He is waiting to come in.

He is knocking at our heart's door showing that He is actively seeking to come in to us. Either we have to open up to Him or we have to ignore Him. He desires entrance so He continues to knock, pleading for us to open the door to our heart so He can come in and fellowship with us and penetrate our entire life forever.

We know all this either in our heads, in which case it will have little impact on us, or we know it by faith in our hearts. However, we also know there are things we want from this world, so we are afraid to let go completely; in which case, it is essential we spend time in His presence to grow in Christ's likeness.

Christ's promises to the overcomer: The overcomers will sit on the throne of Christ. This means we shall rule and reign with Christ forever. We will be assigned duties and responsibilities in helping to oversee the universe. We shall rule and oversee the work of angels. We will rule and reign throughout the whole universe for all eternity as sons and daughters of God and as kings with Christ.

THE CHURCH TODAY

We have completed our look at what Christ had to say to the seven typical churches—churches that represent all the churches that have existed down through the ages.

I believe these seven different types of churches all exist today. I believe each church in existence today has the main characteristics of one of these typical churches. I also believe that each church today has blends and hews of some of the characteristics of the other types of churches mixed into their main type of characteristics.

We need to look at the characteristics of our own church, and match our characteristics with a majority of characteristics from one of these seven types of churches described by Christ. I believe the churches in America today are a mixture of many of those seven churches.

This requires serious and honest soul searching in the presence of Christ. I suggest we need to put all spiritual arrogance aside in our investigation because there are very few churches of Philadelphia in America today, even though many churches today believe they represent the church of Philadelphia.

After identifying which of the seven typical churches our own church resembles, and we get a sense of the hews and blends of the characteristics of the others, we will then know Christ's instructions, His commendations, warnings, counsel and promises to us. We will then know what we have to do. This will all take courage and deep honesty before the Lord.

I would like to give a special word to pastors. Christ's message is directed to you as one of the seven candlesticks (ministers) held in His right hand, His hand of power and might, in the midst of the seven churches. Pastor, you have an awesome responsibility to Christ; He chose you specifically. You must take courage and be brave in Christ; He has left a remnant of the faithful for you in your church, and all of you must stand in His strength as you heed His counsel and warnings.

What is the state of the church today? According to Christ's message to us, the true church will be facing persecutions, especially from the religious community, because the true church stands for Christ just as the church of Smyrna and of Philadelphia. The true church will not be a popular church and will face many obstacles from the religious community. The true church must get its strength from being in, and staying in, the presence of Christ.

The true church more than likely will not be a large congregation in one building, but it must find and network with other true churches.

The state of the church in America today does not seem very encouraging, and there is a temptation for some to become negative toward it. However, there are more people coming to Christ in this generation than in any other. Millions of people around the world each year are committing their lives to Christ. We simply are not seeing that kind of harvest in America yet, but it will come.

God's Word tells us that evil and darkness will abound more and more as we approach the nearness of Christ's return. The task Christ gives us while we are here on earth is to take His light to those lost souls living in the darkness so they have an opportunity to make a choice between Satan or eternal life with Christ.

The state of the church must be that it is ready to be the light of Christ, to give and to be a testimony, to withstand the persecutions and the criticisms coming from the darkness, especially the religious darkness, and to be ready to lead the lost souls to Christ. This must be the state of the true church.

WHERE WE HAVE COME TO

WHERE WE HAVE BEEN

We have come a long way. We have seen the model
God has provided at MCI and looked at the missing piece
in the transformation of our lives, churches and cities. We
have looked at the patterns God has provided for us to
come into His presence and we have seen that when we
get the pattern right, His glorious presence will fall on us.
We have looked at some critical issues that we must address and we have looked at our relationships to other
human beings. We have also looked at what Jesus Christ
has to say to the different types of churches that have existed down through the centuries and how our own church
today is represented among those churches Christ addressed. He is talking to us today.

The MCI model has been especially helpful in that it
has shown us an example in America where a small city, a
men's prison, can be changed.

The model has taught us much, not the least of which

is that the desperation in the lives of many of the inmates left them at a place where they were ready to surrender to Christ.

One of the main purposes of Christ allowing all the disasters to take place during the endtimes will be to make people desperate; it is through their desperation that many people will turn to Him. This is what we have seen in the lives of many inmates at MCI.

Some people refer to what has happened at MCI as "jailhouse religion"; the fact remains, when people are desperate, they turn to Christ. *An extremely valuable lesson here is that we do not have to come to the same desperation, if we will just willingly and honestly, with our entire being, submit ourselves to Jesus Christ.*

It is not necessary for us physically to reach the point of hitting bottom, but we do have to recognize that we must hit bottom spiritually; we must cry out for mercy and grace from our Lord Jesus Christ. *We must desperately seek Him because we love Him and not because of what He can do for us.*

We also learned from the MCI model that it is not necessary for everyone to be on board in order to bring about change. A climate, or atmosphere, can be changed with a dedicated few who pray fervently and who bring the light of the gospel into an area. The light drives back darkness and when it becomes stronger, it begins to push the darkness out. The light still needs to be stronger at MCI. Darkness has an open door through new inmates continually being transferred into the prison, while many inmates who had been bringing light get released.

Another important lesson learned from MCI has been that an informal leadership that is strong in the Lord and committed can be instrumental in bringing about change; inmates are not permitted to hold any formal leadership positions or formal positions of authority in the prison. However, informal leadership definitely exists there, just as it exists in every organizational structure.

We have also learned from the MCI model that there

are those incarcerated who are not interested in, or who do not have a relationship with, Jesus Christ. What they are interested in is making their own life easier. However, they are often drawn to the Lord when they experience non-judgmentalness, see and feel Christ's unconditional love through His vessels and see the hope others have.

It is all right for the uncommitted to test the waters by being involved with the Christian programs; however, it is those inmates who are strong in the Lord and who exercise informal Christian leadership at MCI who prevent the unbelievers and uncommitted to dominate the Christian climate with their own ideas or message.

Unbelievers and uncommitted Christians dominating the climate with their own ideas or message was the grievance Christ had against some of the churches in the book of Revelation, especially the churches of Sardis and Laodicea which were the two churches for which He had no commendation.

We have heard the testimonies of a few "on-fire" and strong-in-the-Lord Christian inmates. These testimonies should be the desire of any pastor. They should also make many pastors somewhat nervous. What would some pastors do with a church full of on-fire, sold-out believers? It may sound exciting at first and it may sound just like what the pastor thinks he needs. The reality is, most churches would definitely have to change from humdrum routine, to the new excitement; people do not like to change and that includes pastors. Pastors would have to learn to pastor that kind of excitement and would have to deal with the complaints from the congregation.

In Proverbs 14:4, we are told that *we can have much increase in production from having oxen, but if we have an ox, we are going to have a mess to clean up.*

Many churches have no idea how they would clean up the messes caused by having some strong-in-the-Lord, on-fire, enthusiastic oxen like the ones whose testimonies we read in chapters two and three. Therefore, the leadership opts for the mundane, unenthusiastic church life where worship and work are kept under tight control. Whatever it is they opt for, they just do not want a mess to clean up, so they do not permit oxen to function in their church.

WHERE HAS OUR JOURNEY BROUGHT US?

We have come to the place in our journey of being able to see there are many different methodologies and combinations of methodologies, as well as organizational structures available to those desiring to transform their city.

We have noted that finding the right strategy or methodology was not the problem. The problem lies in the hearts of the appliers—are they in Christ's presence or in their own?

We thank George Otis for his work in identifying the common elements found in those cities in different countries that are being transformed. The common elements Otis[1] identified are persevering leadership, fervent and united prayer, social reconciliation, public power encounters and diagnostic research.

THE ELEMENTS APPLIED AT MCI

We have seen in the Marion Correctional Institution model what the Otis elements actually look like. For example, persevering leadership is seen in the warden's continual leadership commitment to bring hope, to make a difference and to facilitate and shepherd what is taking place at MCI. It is also seen in the informal leadership of a number of gang leaders by their being intent on staying in the presence of the Lord, putting biblical principles to work and seeking Him passionately because of how much they love Him.

An example of fervent, united prayer is seen at MCI in the persevering prayer of intercessors from the very early stages to current time.

An example of social reconciliation is seen at MCI by the increased communications of different gang leaders with each other and by an increase in positive relationships between many of the inmates and many of the correction officers.

No diagnostic research has taken place at MCI other than the normal statistical reports required of a prison.

An example of public power encounters is seen through healings that have taken place because of God answering prayer and extending His grace. Public power encounters are the confronting of the powers of darkness publicly.

A number of examples of public power encounters have taken place in the popular Experiencing God class at MCI (not to be confused with the popular book by Henry Blackaby and Claude King). Several of those experiences will be discussed here.

In one example, hands were laid on the face of one inmate and relief of pain from tooth cavities was prayed for. The inmate fell under the power of God and while he was on the floor another inmate who was sitting along the side of the room, and who had never been to the class before, said, "Hey! I've got to tell you guys something! While you were praying for him, my knee was healed!" This new attendee to the class had arrived at our class with a swollen knee; he was due to have surgery for it very soon. The swelling in the knee was completely gone and he was able to jump around and walk without his crutches. In addition, the inmate who had the pain from bad teeth was up and he no longer had any pain.

Another example of a public power encounter was an inmate coming into the Experiencing God class on crutches and with a swollen ankle from a bad sprain. *Two other inmates from the class laid their hands on the swollen ankle, rebuked the enemy and prayed for healing. God granted their prayer request and the young man's swelling disappeared and he danced around the room giving praise to Jesus.*

Another public power encounter example at MCI was an inmate class member coming to an Experiencing God class and he was unable to move his head, shoulder or arm due to a herniated disk in his neck. The herniated disk had him immobilized in those areas and he was in great pain. The entire class laid hands on this inmate, rebuked the demonic and prayed for healing. At the conclusion of the prayer, this inmate began very carefully to move his head, then he began to turn his head and move his shoulder and then he raised his whole arm. He could do none of this before without excruciating pain and the pain was gone. The herniated disk itself was not healed and later that year this same inmate had an operation to correct the situation.

Many of the inmates involved in the examples of these public power encounters had not yet given their lives to the Lord. However, most of them, as well as many others, did so very shortly after their experience with God in their lives.

The typical approach used with the MCI Experiencing God class went as follows: First, the outside volunteers came into the prison and prayed over the meeting room, taking authority over the area. They were able to do this because they had been in the presence of the Lord together and were united servants of God.

Second, the team would spend time worshiping the Lord along with the inmates.

Third, in prayer, the team would rebuke the enemy from the meeting room so the eyes and hearts of the inmate class members would be opened to truth.

Fourth, the team would take testimonies of how God had worked in the life of the inmates the previous week.

Fifth, the team would present the Word of God to the inmates.

Sixth, the team would offer opportunities for class members to come to the Lord.

Lastly, the team would offer ministry and healing to the inmates.

On occasion, there would be a particular need and the Lord would intervene and change everything. The point is the Lord was in charge of the methodology.

The volunteers, who included me, conducting the Experiencing God class at MCI, walked into the prison in the presence of the Lord. In addition, we were united in prayer and in purpose. There was a balance between being in the presence of God and doing His work. Being in the presence of God was a continual experience, and doing His work was simply responding in faith to what the Lord put in front of us that particular week at the prison.

As a part of the volunteer team, I can say without any qualification that when the team entered the prison and we walked through the halls to our classroom area, the enemy knew we were there, and we could sense the enemy parting out of our way. We know this because we walked in the authority of the Lord, doing His work, after being in His presence. As a result, He allowed us to be a part of the lives that were given hope and being changed.

WHERE DO WE GO FROM HERE?

Do you want to see God change your city or your church? The common questions I hear in conferences across America are, "How do we bring revival? How do we bring heaven to earth? How do we welcome in the King of Glory?"

The major key to city or church transformation is having a personal transformation.

For God to change your city or your church, you must first have a radical transformation yourself. If you want to usher in a major move of God, you must first have a God encounter yourself.

Several years ago, on a mission trip to Argentina, I had the opportunity to speak personally to the great evangelist Carlos Annacondia. I told him it was easy being an "on-fire" Christian in the mission field, because everyone around was on fire for the Lord, the anointing was strong and the expectations were high. However, it was not easy to maintain that anointed spirit back in America. *In America, the battle rages with the enemy and there is an oppressive spirit. The expectations in America are low. Most Americans' self-sufficiency is strong and they do not believe they need anything except what they can get for themselves from the world.*

The response Annacondia gave me is important for all

reading this book to ponder. He said you must find a way to give the anointing away. *He said the anointing has a purpose, and that purpose is to give the anointing away; it is not for me or for him personally to hold on to. It must be given to others or we will lose it.*

Annacondia cited Isaiah 61, which states, *"the Spirit of the Sovereign Lord is on me, because the Lord has anointed me to preach good news to the poor. He has sent me to bind up the broken hearted, to proclaim freedom for the captives and release from darkness for the prisoners, to proclaim the year of the Lord's favor."* This is the purpose of the anointing; it is to be used for other people.

Annacondia also cited 2 Kings 4:1-7 which is about the widow who had very little oil for cooking and was told to take what she had and fill all the empty jars she could find. The oil continued to flow as long as the widow poured it into empty jars. When she could find no more empty jars to fill, the oil stopped flowing; it dried up.

The analogy in 2 Kings is obvious. The oil represents the anointing of the Holy Spirit. The widow pouring the oil represents our giving the anointing of the Holy Spirit on our lives away to those who are empty. When the widow found no more empty jars, or empty people, to give the anointing to, the anointing stopped flowing.

According to Annacondia, the same thing happens to us and it causes us to lose the anointing. We may have tried to keep it for ourselves or we just may not have looked hard enough for those who need it. We may not want to get out of our comfort zone and would rather bask in our own personal enjoyment of the anointing. We just may not work hard enough to find a way to give the anointing away to those in need.

Annacondia said we must look for the needy and the hurting to whom we may give the anointing. We must invite them to dinner, we must meet their needs and we must tell them about Jesus. We must do whatever it takes to get to know the needy and hurting so we can give them the anointing of Jesus. We must look for family members, neighbors and co-workers to give the anointing. *No matter what else we do, we must find a way to give away what God has given to us.* Why? Because we love Jesus Christ.

Finding and associating with the needy, the lost and the hurting is not easy for those of us who associate almost exclusively with Christians and church members. We may work around non-Christians but usually have very little to do with them socially.

At MCI, our Experiencing God team went to the prison each week for a number of years and we earned the trust of the inmates. Other volunteer groups would come to the prison much less often and on irregular visits. The inmates would go see what they could get from the volunteers, like food or Bibles or whatever. The volunteers would leave feeling good about themselves for their good work and the inmates would chuckle because they got "goodies," but had to give no trust or commitment in return.

I worked in an inner city church for a season and it took the consistent love of Christ to win trust and truly to be able to minister to inner city people. On occasion the suburban churches would come into the inner city bringing gifts of food and clothing and other handouts; the inner-city folks would take everything they could get, but in return they gave no trust and they gave no commitment; as a result, their lives were not changed.

If we are going to make a difference in the lives of needy and hurting people, we must be willing to change our life-style to associate with the needy and hurting and to develop positive relationships with them that build trust over time.

Those in America's churches who are complacent, self-sufficient and self-satisfied are also in need; they just do not know it or will not admit it, and that makes them difficult to reach. They need to see value in giving away what God has given them. For that reason they need to see us demonstrate going to where we can find, and where we can relate to, the hurting and needy. *When we are willing to do that, when we walk our talk, we will earn the right to be heard by the complacent church attendee.*

The harvest is so great that it is imperative to find and train workers. Where will these workers come from? In America, most will come from the complacent, self-sufficient, self-satisfied people in churches. How will that happen? We must earn the right to be heard by them through our commitment to, and implementation of, ministry to the needy and hurting. When the church members see that and are given an opportunity to participate in something much larger than themselves, many will be eager to become involved.

Many of the hurting and needy in the inner city are so socially and emotionally deprived that it will take a long time to transform them into productive harvesters, but we dare not ignore them. There are precious jewels that can come from that segment of society, and they can reach others that we could never reach. *Due to the shortness of the hour and the desperate need for workers, the church is the best place to look for those workers that can soon qualify as disciples to teach others. We must use whatever means possible to activate those potential workers.* Providing instruction and opportunities for practice within the local church would seem the most prudent way to cultivate workers.

MAKING DISCIPLES

Christ commanded us to go and make disciples. How do we do that? The same way Christ did. When Christ found a person willing to learn and willing to commit his life to God, Christ attached Himself to that person. Christ modeled what He wanted that person to learn and to do. He began to mold and to make that person into His image. The disciple watched, helped and took on the character of Christ.

The word attached is the key word that best describes discipleship.

Christ made disciples by attaching Himself to them, and through that personal attachment, they were able to observe His life, His ministry and His relationship with the Father. In being with Him, seeing Him and hearing

Him they began to take on His life and character. This is how Christ made disciples. This is also to be our mission and our method, to attach ourselves to willing believers; this is how we are to make disciples.

The catch is, we must be in the presence of Christ, just as Christ was in the presence of the Father. We must learn to be in constant prayer and to fast for the lost souls in a way that Christ fasted, by becoming so absorbed in His plea to the Father for the lost that He did not take time to eat. That needs to be our hunger just as it was the hunger of Christ.

Even though we live, eat, work and play in this world, we must learn to do it all while in the constant presence of Christ; that is the only way we will see what He is doing so we can join Him in faith. *We must intentionally set out to practice making Christ the center of our universe rather than ourselves. This will not happen without intentional effort on our part and without being truly in love with Jesus.*

When we live, walk and have our being in Christ, rather than ourselves, our whole life takes on a different focus. We will not have to stop to pray and fast when confronted with an emergency ministry need like the disciples faced in trying to cast a demon out of a little boy while Christ was up on the Mount of Transfiguration. *We must be ready to minister at all times through constant prayer and fasting for the lost, the hurting and the needy.*

Our efforts in transforming our cities and our churches have had, for the most part, its focus on the world's way of developing and implementing vision. The focus has been on the doing of the vision rather than on the being in His presence while we are in the act of doing the work. In addition, our focus must be on Jesus because we are in love with Him and not because of what He can do for us. We have been out of balance.

Christ's Presence

Being in Christ's presence is an easy thing to say and it is an easy thing to take for granted. We think we are in

His presence because we are good, practicing Christians, we love the Lord and we pray often; however, *it takes a determined, continuous effort to stay in the presence of the Lord. It does not just happen because we are good people, love the Lord, do good things and because we were in the presence of Christ when we sought His direction yesterday or last week or even last month or longer.*

We all have a human nature, and daily we must sacrifice it at the cross; it may even need to be sacrificed more often, depending upon the depth of our bad habits and desires. First John 1:8 says that *if we say we have no sin the truth is not in us and we deceive ourselves, and if we claim we have not sinned we make Him out to be a liar.*

We will all be in a raging war with our flesh until Christ takes us home or until He returns. We dare not let our guard down by not staying in His presence or by thinking that it was enough to be in His presence when we sought direction for where we should go or what we should do.

However, I am afraid that many people reason that now, since we have the answer from Him, we need to get on with figuring out how to do what He said. This kind of thinking does not bring balance between being in His presence and doing His work; this kind of thinking has tended to get the institutional church into a mess.

THE INSTITUTIONAL CHURCH

We must recognize that the institutional church in America is broken. The sad thing is that the institutional church is full of people who truly believe they are fine because they do all the Christian things the church tells them they need to do, and because they really are good people.

A key tactic of the institutional church is its inward focus, its focus on its own self rather than focusing on the great commission of going out to the world.

The church membership needs to be a part of reaching out to the lost and hurting. Doing this effectively requires being in the presence of Christ. When church members reach outside their own selves and their own church's four walls, they are being a part of something much bigger than themselves and that gives meaning and excitement to life.

The Christian researcher, George Barna, gives some eye opening insight into the state of the church today. This is important because it demonstrates how out of balance we are between being in His presence and doing His work.

According to Barna[2], nearly 50% of protestant pastors today do not have a Christian worldview; that means there is some part of the foundational basics of Scripture they do not believe.

Those basics of Scripture identified by Barna are that Jesus Christ is God incarnated by the Virgin Mary; that He lived a sinless life; that He died on the cross for our sins so we could be reconciled to God the Father and so we could spend eternity in heaven; that He was raised from the dead and that He ascended into heaven and that He will return.

It is astounding, and frightening, that 50% of American protestant pastors do not believe some part of these foundational basics of Scripture.

If nearly 50% of the pastors do not believe in some part of the basic and essential foundation of Scripture, where does that leave the church members? We know where it leaves them—in a wilderness, in a broken church, and for the most part, thinking they are eternally secure because they are good people. *According to Barna[3], 91% of all born-again Christians—not just those people who call themselves Christian—do not believe in some part of the foundational basics of Scripture.*

Is it any wonder that the morality of America continues to decline with the number of unchurched adults nearly doubling since 1991 and spiritual progress being difficult to find?

Is it any wonder we have had such little success in transforming our churches and cities?

In the past, the church in America has provided the wall of protection around our lives. However, as in Nehemiah, the walls around our lives and cities have been seriously damaged and they must be rebuilt.

Because of our broken church walls, we are not adequately able to protect those we love and care for. We have been ineffective and that must change.

James 1:13-15 (NLT)

And remember, no one who wants to do wrong should ever say, "God is tempting me." God is never tempted to do wrong, and he never tempts anyone else either. 14Temptation comes from the lure of our own evil desires. 15These evil desires lead to evil actions, and evil actions lead to death.

INTRODUCTION

As a church, we have responsibility for our own section of the wall to rebuild, just as in the book of Nehemiah. We do not have to be Nehemiah, but we do need to collaborate and cooperate with others who are also working on the wall; if we do not, when it comes time to connect our section of the wall with another section, the parts may not meet or match.

This does not mean that we are just to collaborate and cooperate with other churches in our own denomination. It means we must collaborate and cooperate with churches from different denominations in our city. The Body of Christ cannot be separated.

I would like simply to list some of the concepts mentioned in this book as a summary for you; these concepts need to be internalized. There are many more concepts covered in the book that are not listed below, but these should provide a basic starting place for transformation of our cities. I will then close with what I believe are minimum recommendations to get on the right path for transformation.

CONCEPTS

→ Start by falling deeply and desperately in love with Jesus.

→ Get around others who are desperately in love with Jesus. If you cannot find people like that, then help those in your sphere of influence to fall desperately in love with Him.

→ Learn to follow God's prescribed pattern to come into His presence. This must be learned and practiced. We must follow the temple pattern and we must take every word of Second Chronicles 7:14 to heart and not just let it settle in our heads. *"If My people, who are called by My name, will humble themselves and pray and seek My face and turn from their wicked way, then I will hear from heaven and will forgive their sin and will heal their land."*

→ To transform a city today we must build a sanctuary, a sacred place, within ourselves so God will come and dwell among us.

→ Intentionally begin to practice staying in His presence as you go about your day. Look at what God is putting in front of you and ask what He wants you to do or say. Ask Him to open your eyes to see and your ears to hear what He is doing and saying.

→ ***There must be a balance between our being in the presence of God and our doing His work.***

→ There must be a determined effort to reach out to other churches in our city; churches with whom we can agree on the foundational absolutes discussed in chapter nine. Seeking to find, and to hook up with, other kingdom people are priorities. The kingdom people are there; we just have to make a concerted effort to find them and to connect with them.

→ It is also necessary to take the time to develop relationships with kingdom people. Consider prayer groups or a pastor/leader prayer summit.

→ Remember the MCI model. It was never the intention to transform MCI; *it was the intention to bring hope to the inmates through the love and light of Christ, and the inmates fell in love with Jesus.* Prison officials from other prisons have adopted the programs at MCI; however, their focus has been on changing their own prison and not on bringing hope to inmates through Christ's love; that has been secondary, if considered at all. *This focus is subtle but critical, and it makes the difference between a changed and an unchanged prison or city.* The other prison officials have had a variety of different reasons to institute procedures similar to MCI, not the least of which has been the desire of the State Director of the Department of Rehabilitation and Corrections. This has put a strong but subtle pressure on other prisons to perform as well as MCI.

→ Find the needs that can be cooperatively worked on together, and determine to bring light into the city, person by person.

→ Constantly seek the presence of the Lord, seeking to walk in His Spirit. He wants to be in our presence more than we want to be in His. *Make the people in your church aware of the pattern God has provided for coming into His presence.*

→ Diligently seek a life of righteousness. Our being in Christ is what causes God to count us as righteous. Being righteous is not something we can do ourselves, so we must seek to be in His presence.

→ Begin to develop discipleship material for attaching ourselves to those committed to following Christ.

→ Study the MCI model.

→ Determine some specific acts that can be done personally, or jointly, to change the spiritual climate.

→ Begin to look for what needs to be changed within our own self first, before we try to change what is outside of us, in our environment. *If we are not transformed ourselves, we cannot transform our church or our city.*

→ Be sure we are cooperating and working with those who believe in the absolutes of scripture.

→ Be certain that God has selected the key leadership. God chooses the most unlikely people for leadership; He does that so others will know He is the One responsible for any success in reaching people in our cities.

→ The leadership must be willing to be broken before God and totally submitted to Him; they must be willing to be obedient and walk through all doors opened by God.

→ *The core leadership must individually and corporately build a sanctuary, a sacred place, so God's presence will come and habitat with them—not just come and visit.*

→ We must train and discipline ourselves in faith. We must copy that great cloud of witnesses in Hebrews 11, who went before us to show the way and to show us what could be done, that cloud of witnesses who are cheering us on now, because they were people just like us and they are watching from heaven.

→ Be aware of group issues such as power and influence and the different stages of group growth, and do not allow group members to get caught in conflict. Also, be aware that the enemy will use these tension points as entryways to create division. All this takes courage to deal with, when it would be much easier to just walk away from the group effort.

→ We need to intentionally be carriers of Christ's message to the churches, which is found in the book of Revelation. It seems as though we should not have to take the message to the churches, but the reality is, we do have to in the vast majority of them.

→ We need to intentionally carry the message of hope to the churches so the broken walls around our families and city can be repaired.

→ Many of the institutional churches today teach both love and fluff; not many teach war and polarization. There needs to be balance in the teaching. The imbalance that exists today leaves us handicapped in understanding the times in which we live.

→ Attach yourself to a potential disciple who wants to learn and grow in Christ.

There is not a prescribed procedure or plan to follow for bringing about transformation. It is necessary to seek the Lord, to come into His presence, and to learn to stay there. This way we will be ready at any time to do the work of Christ. It is necessary to be desperately in love with Jesus. Unfortunately, many people are more in love with what they are doing or who they are, than they are desperate for Jesus.

We know what it takes to bring the presence of Christ. It takes humility, fervent prayer, unity with others and holiness in our lives. However, when we look at the results of our knowing how to invite the presence of God, we find it just does not happen much in America. The reason is that we usually only invite His presence into our heads and not into our hearts. The information is just information in our heads and we have not internalized to the point where we act on what we know.

We just do not pursue the presence of God with a reckless abandon. We do not let everything go so we can seek God. We have not been willing to stop what we are doing and put everything on hold until we have heard from God. We must be willing to abandon what we are doing, as well as our own priorities, in order to be His people and to be called by His name.

Do other people know that those of us who desire His presence are really His people? Do they know we are called by His name, by His identity or authority? Or, do they know us by some other name such as: pastor, deacon, chairman of the church board, community leader, city-reaching committee member, etc., or by whatever other name we have allowed ourselves to be known?

Are any of us called the man or woman of God?

We know very well, for example, what Second Chronicles 7:14 says; we have it memorized and we even pray it. "If" we will do the things God says, "then" He will hear from heaven and forgive our sin and heal our land. Why has this not happened in America?

It has not happened in America because we have not

abandoned ourselves, we have not been willing to set aside our own agendas and life priorities. We have not fulfilled what God has said we need to do. We have not truly been His people; rather, we have been our own persons. We have not truly been called by His name; rather, we are usually called by our position or by what we do. The four things God says we must do, just never seem to all be put together at once—we just never seem to get there. This is evident by God not fulfilling His part. **IF** we will humble ourselves, pray, seek His face and turn from our wickedness, **THEN**, and only then, will He heal our land. This is God's promise and His promises are true. *No amount of rationalization can avoid acknowledging the fact that something is wrong with our part and not God's.* What else could be the explanation for God not moving in America as He is moving in other countries?

RECOMMENDATIONS

In addition to internalizing the concepts in this book, I believe we need to be doing the following:

1. *First and foremost, be sure we "know" Jesus—not just know "about" Jesus. For this to be possible, we must spend time with Him in prayer, talking with Him. We must learn His Word, and we must meditate on His Word so it sinks into our spirit and not just settle in our heads.* There is no shortcut for this, no matter how talented or gifted we are and no matter what kind of position we hold.

2. We must fall in love with Jesus. If we love ourselves, or someone else or anything else, more than Jesus, we are wasting our time and any success we have will come only from our own strength; we may have a lot of personal strength and talent, but it will have its limit.

3. Learn to come into the presence of the Lord. This takes practice and we need to understand the pattern of the tabernacle—which is knowing we only get into the presence through Jesus.

4. Music is fine—and I love worship music— however,

if we rely on music to bring us into the presence of the Lord, what are we going to do when we meet someone in need on the street, or at the grocery store and we need to be anointed, but we have no music to get us into His presence? We need to learn to walk daily in the Spirit of the Lord. This takes intentional and continual practice.

5. It is not enough to know in our head what it takes to bring the presence of Christ. We must intentionally, without reservation, and with reckless abandon, seek after Him with all our being.

6. *We must abandon everything to seek Christ, not for what He can do for us but because we are desperately in love with Him. This calls for some major attitude changes in most of us.*

7. We must believe and know that we are His people. We are not someone else's, such as our spouses, our employers or ourselves.

8. We must be called by His name. We cannot be closet Christians; we cannot be ashamed to be known as a strong Christian; we must be willing to let the world know we walk in the name of Jesus Christ.

9. We must not use the excuse that we will turn away the people of the world whom we are trying to impact if we are intentional about being in Christ.

10. We must remember those men at Marion Correctional Institution who have hope, joy, peace and righteousness, and it is that which has brought transformation to MCI. It has not been a fantastic strategy, program or vision. It has been the recognition of the supremacy of Christ, being in His presence, falling in love with Him, and then finding ways to meet needs and extend hope with whatever meager means have been available. God has honored these efforts.

11. We must be willing to stop whatever we are doing to seek revelation from God and how He wants us to proceed. This means that pastors must also be willing to do this no matter how busy they are.

12. *At home, we must not allow ourselves to be*

sleepy eyed or routine with our devotions and prayers,
but we must passionately seek Him in our reading
and in our prayer.

13. Pastor, you need to assess whether you spend as much time in pursuing the great commission as you do on programming, growing your church or controlling what goes on at your church. A true assessment here will tell you much about what kind of church you have in the eyes of Christ.

14. Congregation member, if you have a passion for reaching the lost and transforming your city, but your pastor does not seem supportive, seek his blessing first, then initiate reaching the lost; he will most likely be grateful.

15. Congregation member, if your pastor tells you that your vision or desire is not his vision for the church, find out exactly what his vision is, how it is being achieved and how you can fit in or help. If his vision does not include, as a centerpiece, the fulfilling of the great commission, then you have a choice to make.

16. Seek like-minded people. You will find them by networking with other churches, ministries and Christian business people in the marketplace and government. You will find them almost any place you go and look for them.

17. If possible, bring in city-reaching consultants to assist with the process—after you have been in the presence of the Lord and know you have fallen in love with Jesus.

18. *There is a desperate need to keep a balance between being in the presence of Christ and doing His work. A major problem in America is being out of balance by placing the emphasis on the doing; it just subtly slips in without our realizing it.*

Summary

There are over 180 different cities in America in some stage of the process of city-reaching and the number is growing. So, for those who desire to see their city transformed, there are many different strategies available to look at and study. Most of these strategies can be molded, adapted, expanded or changed to fit the particular needs of your city.

It will not be difficult to develop a plan to fit your city. It is important that the final plan originates from your core leadership and that they all take ownership of it.

The major problem so far has not been with the plan; it has been that people begin to implement their plan in their own strength or they allow their focus to become centered on something other than giving God glory.

There is no short-term solution to transformation. The solution takes time. It takes falling in love with Jesus, learning to come into His presence, learning to believe and have faith. It also takes learning to develop His character and to walk this life by following His commands. As our efforts go forward, we must also be aware of the issues of group growth, as well as power and influence, so that we may be aware of the schemes the enemy will try to use against us.

After all the above takes place, then it takes organization, skill, determined perseverance and time to implement God's revelation.

In ending this book, I would like to express that my desire has been to bring God glory through this work, to bring more of His beloved people into His presence and to learn to dwell there.

I believe with all my heart that MCI was given to us as a gift from God to show the absolute necessity of being in love with Jesus and coming into His presence.

I also believe, based on Christ's message to us in the book of Revelation, that evil, darkness, deterioration of morality and the coldness of man's heart is bound to increase. Therefore, I believe our call to change the city is a call to change the individual lives within the city, by giving those who will accept, the hope and light of Jesus Christ and of eternal life.

A survey[1] done with local leadership of cities in some stage of transformation asked the question "What obstacles does your City Movement face?" The response ranked highest was a lack of participation. Second, third and fourth all ranked nearly the same and just under the "lack of participation" response. Second was "racial/ethnic division"; third was "denominational division"; and fourth was "ego—lack of humility."

Let us look at these results for a minute. The issues of racial/ethnic division and denominational division both deal with relationships, and the issue of ego, or lack of humility, deals with the improper use of power when one lacks humility. These three issues then lead to the first issue of a lack of participation. People either never join the citywide effort or they do so tentatively, until one of the three issues surfaces, then they withdraw, or they just do not join any citywide effort at all.

I believe if we could solve the racial/ethnic issue, the denominational division issue and the ego, or lack of humility issue, we would solve what was identified as the major issue of lack of participation.

Do I know how to solve these problems? No. And neither does anyone else. However, God knows how to solve the problems and that is where we have to turn.

The missing piece has been summed up in this book as being in God's presence on a continual basis and having Him send us to do His work. *When we are ready to get serious about changing our cities and changing America, we will dedicate the time required to truly humble ourselves corporately, truly seek His face, truly pray with passion and cry out to Him for grace and mercy and truly turn from our wicked ways. Then, and only then, will God hear from heaven and heal our land.*

Somewhere in this land of America—in some city—we will find a remnant of people who will become willing to do what the inmates did at Marion Correctional Institution, that is, abandon themselves, submit to the Lord and stay in His presence. Until we do that, it is unlikely that He will send us to work as He did the inmates.

There is no way that humans are going to break the strongholds of racial/ethnic division and denominational division in America without being in the presence of God and learning to see what He is doing and hear what He is saying.

I firmly believe that if it is not God's timing for cities to be transformed in America, we may expend all our energy, gifts, and talents and it still will not happen.

However, I also firmly believe He has provided us with the MCI model for a reason, and that reason is to let us know it is, truly, His timing for American cities. It is time for the demonic strongholds of racism and denominational division to be broken from our cities and from our lives.

I believe that through the MCI model and through this book, He is reinforcing the need for us to learn to come into His presence following the patterns He has provided.

This will not be easy, and it will require a life-style change on our part. It must be intentional on our part because living a life-style that follows God's patterns just is not how most Americans live.

I have included for your assistance under this note[2] in the endnotes for this chapter a number of web sites that will give you a sense for how the city-reaching movement is progressing.

God bless you and your efforts to bring His Kingdom into your life, your workplace, your church and your city. I would be privileged to be of help in your efforts in any way you think I might be able. If I can help you in your journey toward transformation by presenting seminars, workshops or speaking, I would be happy to discuss your particular needs with you. You may see the Contact Information at the end of the book.

Romans 12:4-5 (NLT)

Just as our bodies have many parts and each part has a special function, ⁵so it is with Christ's body. We are all parts of his one body, and each of us has different work to do. And since we are all one body in Christ, we belong to each other, and each of us needs all the others.

John 17:20-23 (NLT)

"I am praying not only for these disciples but also for all who will ever believe in me because of their testimony. ²¹My prayer for all of them is that they will be one, just as you and I are one, Father—that just as you are in me and I am in you, so they will be in us, and the world will believe you sent me.

²²"I have given them the glory you gave me, so that they may be one, as we are—²³I in them and you in me, all being perfected into one. Then the world will know that you sent me and will understand that you love them as much as you love me."

Endnotes

John 13:34-35 (NLT)

So now I am giving you a new commandment: Love each other. Just as I have loved you, you should love each other. [35] Your love for one another will prove to the world that you are my disciples.

Matthew 25:36 (NLT)

I was naked, and you gave me clothing. I was sick, and you cared for me. I was in prison, and you visited me.

ENDNOTES

CHAPTER 1

1. http://www.promisekeepers.org/paffnews260
   "Promise Keepers Goes to Jail." August 8, 2003

2. "Locks" and "Dorms" are where the inmates live
   at MCI. Locks have individual cells with two
   beds in each cell in bunk-bed style. Dorms are
   open areas, or dormitories, with all the bunk beds
   lined up along the walls. There are an equal
   number of locks and dorms to house the 1,800
   men.

3. http://www.drc.state.oh.us/web/Articles/
   article98.htm "Prisoners Reentering Society:
   Revisiting the Transition From Incarceration to
   the Community." (Paper prepared for Third
   National Forum on Restorative Justice, spon-
   sored by Justice Fellowship, Orlando, Florida,
   March 14-16, 2002.) Director Reginald A.
   Wilkinson, Ed.D., Director
   Ohio Department of Rehabilitation and
   Correction.

4. http://www.citreach.org/index.html

CHAPTER 8

1. *New Unger's Bible Dictionary.* Merrill F. Unger.
   The Moody Bible Institute of Chicago, 1988
   Revised and Updated Edition. P. 236.

2. Ted Haggard. *Primary Purpose.* Creation House.
   600 Rinehart Road, Lake Mary, FL 32746.
   pp.54-64.

3. *Informed Intercession: Transforming Your Community Through Spiritual Mapping and Strategic Prayer.* George Otis, Jr. Renew Books, A Division of Gospel Light. Ventura, California. 1999. p. 55.

CHAPTER 9

1. George O. Charrier. "COG'S Ladder: A Model of Group Growth." *S.A.M. Advance Management Journal* 37:30-37. Jan. 1972.

CHAPTER 10

1. French, J. R. P., and Raven, B. 1959. "The Bases of Social Power." In *Studies in Social Power,* ed. D. Cartwright. Ann Arbor: University of Michigan, Institute for Social Research.

2. Raven, B. H., and Kruglanski, W. 1975. "Conflict and Power." In the *Structure of Conflict,* Ed. P.G. Swingle, New York, NY: Academic Press, 177-219.

3. Hersey, P. and Goldsmith, M. (April, 1980). "The changing role of performance management." *Training and Development Journal.*

4. Sergiovanni, T. J., and Starrat, R. J. 1998. *Supervision: A Redefinition.* Boston, MA: McGraw-Hill Companies, Inc.

5. Bulach, C. 2000. *Nine Ways Leaders Can Motivate Employees.* http://www.westga.edu/~sclimate/powertypology.htm

6. D. Vincent Ford. 1984. "A Comparison of Principals' Perception of Faculty Influence and Principal's Effectiveness as Perceived by Faculty." *PhD Dissertation.* College of Education, Ohio University. p. 12.

CHAPTER 12

1. *Informed Intercession: Transforming Your Community Through Spiritual Mapping and Strategic Prayer.* George Otis, Jr. Renew Books, A Division of Gospel Light. Ventura, California. 1999. p. 55.

2. George Barna. "Only Half Of Protestant Pastors Have A Biblical Worldview." http:/www.barna.org/FlexPage.aspx?Page=BarnaUpdate&Barna UpdateID=156

3. *Think Like Jesus.* George Barna. Tyndale House Publishers, Inc. Wheaton, Illinois, 60189 2003. p. 39.

CHAPTER 13

1. http://www.myfaith.com/city-impact/leadership-survey.htm

2. Following are a few web sites that will be helpful in letting you know some of the things going on in America in the efforts to bring change to cities.

   a. http://www.transformationthemissingpiece.com

   b. http://www.drbudford.com

   c. http://www.thedwellingplaceministries.com

   d. http://www.dvincentford.com

   e. http://www.citireach.org/

   f. http://www.nppn.org/CIR/CIR%20-%20Bibliography0210.pdf

g. http://www.projectpray.org/cities/compo-
    nents/pastors.html

h. http://www.transformationcincinnati.com/

i. http://missioncolumbus.net/
    city_reaching.htm

j. http://www.cityreaching.com/

k. http://www.citytransformation.org

l. http://www.missionhouston.org/synapse/
    center/
    homepage.cfm?website=missionhouston.org

m. http://www.missionspokane.org/

n. http://www.nppn.org/

o. http://www.radchr.net/LISTS/RadicalChr/
    msg00009.htm

p. http://www.missionamerica.org/
    Brix?pageID=12737

q. http://www.openheaven.com/

r. http://www.floodgatevision.net/
    newsletter.asp

s. http://www.toledoprayernet.com/
    ?GXHC_gx_session_id_FutureTenseContent
    Server=b913417ea97033eb

t. http://www.transformingmelbourne.org/
    key_to.php

u. http://www.cfyc.org/

v. http://www.harvestevan.org/

w. http://www.missionportland.org/

x. http://www.nppn.org/cir.htm

y. http://www.thedwellingplaceministries.com

z. http://www.missionmamivalley.com

Roman 14:17-19 (NLT)

For the Kingdom of God is not a matter of what we eat or drink, but of living a life of goodness and peace and joy in the Holy Spirit. 18If you serve Christ with this attitude, you will please God. And other people will approve of you, too. 19So then, let us aim for harmony in the church and try to build each other up.

1John 5:14-15 (NLT)

And we can be confident that he will listen to us whenever we ask him for anything in line with his will. 15And if we know he is listening when we make our requests, we can be sure that he will give us what we ask for.

Appendices

1. Discipleship Topic Outline One

2. Discipleship Topic Outline Two

3. Sample Lord's Prayer for City Reaches

4. Sample Tabernacle Prayer

Matthew 10:11-15 (NLT)

Whenever you enter a city or village, search for a worthy man and stay in his home until you leave for the next town. ¹²When you are invited into someone's home, give it your blessing. ¹³If it turns out to be a worthy home, let your blessing stand, if it is not, take back the blessing. ¹⁴If a village doesn't welcome you or listen to you, shake off the dust of that place from your feet as you leave. ¹⁵I assure you, the wicked cities of Sodom and Gomarrah will be better off on the judgment day than that place will be.

APPENDIX 1

Discipleship Topic Outline One

1. Foundations
2. Word of God
3. Know Your Enemy
4. Our Weapons
5. Assurance of Salvation
6. Living in Victory
7. Forgiveness
8. Faith
9. Prayer
10. The Holy Spirit
11. Witnessing
12. Love
13. Knowing god's Will
14. Stewardship: Time, Money, Talents
15. Water Baptism
16. Holy communion
17. Divine Healing
18. Heaven
19. Hell
20. Rapture and the Second coming
21. Cults and Religions
22. The Church

Matthew 5:14 (NLT)
You are the light of the world—like a city on a mountain, glowing in the night for all to see.

1 John 5:19 (NLT)
We know that we are children of God and that the world around us is under the power and control of the evil one.

APPENDIX 2

Discipleship Topic Outline Two

1. Relating to God
2. Salvation
3. Forgiveness
4. Learning about God
5. The Christ Relationship
6. The Kingdom of God
7. The Holy Spirit
8. The Christian Life
9. The Future: Rapture, Tribulation, second Coming of Christ, Millennium, New Heavens and New Earth
10. Prayer
11. The Believer's Participation

Deuteronomy 4:29 (NLT)

From there you will search again for the LORD your God. And if you search for him with all your heart and soul, you will find him.

Romans 10:3 (NLT)

For they don't understand God's way of making people right with himself. Instead, they are clinging to their own way of getting right with God by trying to keep the law. They won't go along with God's way.

APPENDIX 3

Sample Lord's Prayer for City Reachers

1. Our Father Which Art In Heaven, Hallowed Be Thy Name

Father, we come before You with thanksgiving in our hearts for You are a great and mighty God. For You have been good to us. We hollow Your name for You are God and God alone. There is none like You. You are high and lifted up and Your train fills the temple.

Father, You are the Alpha and the Omega, our beginning and ending. Every good and perfect thing comes from You. Everything that exists is because of You.

Father, You are our hiding place in times of trouble. You fill our hearts with the song of deliverance. We trust You Lord. In every situation we trust You. Your joy is our strength today and forever. Let the weak say I am strong in the strength of the Lord.

Father, You are great and greatly to be praised in this city. You are the joy of the whole earth. Lord, we lift Your name on high. Lord we thank You for the works You have done in our lives.

We come before You today saying, have mercy on us O' God, according to Your unfailing love.

We hollow Your name today, for You are:

Jehovah-Tsidkenu -	The lord our righteousness
Jehovah-M'kaddesh –	The Lord who sanctifies
Jehovah-Shalom –	The Lord our peace
Jehovah-Shammah –	The Lord is there
Jehovah-Rophe –	The Lord who heals
Jehovah-Jireh –	The Lord's provision shall be seen
Jehovah-Nissi –	The Lord is my banner
Jehovah-Rohi –	The Lord my shepherd
El-Shaddai –	The God Almighty of Bless ings. You are the Mighty Breasted one who nourishes and supplies
Elohim –	The Creator of the heavens and earth who was in the beginning. The earth is Yours and the fullness there of.

2. Thy Kingdom Come, Thy Will Be Done –

In myself, my family, my church, my neighborhood, my city.

Father, we thank you that Your kingdom has come to this city. We thank You that Your kingdom has come to my personal sphere of influence. Your kingdom is not eating or drinking, but righteousness, peace and joy in the Holy Ghost.

We come before you and humble ourselves in prayer and we seek Your face and turn from our wicked ways. We turn from our self-centeredness, pride, selfishness, jealousy, envy, and we ask for Your forgiveness as we ask for Your Kingdom to come in our lives.

Father, we thank You that Your Kingdom has come to our

city. We thank You that Your Kingdom has come to our city by Your being in us and we are in the city.

We thank You that every place the souls of our feet tread around our city You have given to us. We thank You that Your will is being done in our city through Your servants, and we pray for more harvester servants.

Come, let Your Kingdom come and Your will be done in my life!
Come, let Your Kingdom come and Your will be done in the lives of my family!
Come, let Your Kingdom come and Your will be done in my church!
Come, Kingdom of God in our city!
Come, and let Your will be done in our city!

3. Give Us This Day Our Daily Bread

Father, we thank you for Your daily provisions for our city.

We thank You for the citizens who acknowledge You for all their substances.

We thank You for the city maintenance personnel who are upright and moral.

We thank You for honest work and for honest and just government and for integrity at every level of operation in our city.

We thank You for churches in our city that daily honor and acknowledge You.

We thank You for Your Word which is a plumb line for our city.

We thank You Father for Your prosperity in our city, and

for providing gainful employment for those citizens with a mind to work.

We thank You Father, for the work of restoration You are doing in our city, our neighborhoods, our homes and our families.

4. Forgive Us Our Debts As WE Forgive Our Debtors

Father, forgive us our sin. We are called by Your name and we humble ourselves and pray and seek Your face. Hear from heaven and forgive our sin and heal the land.

Father, we confess that we are caught in sin and we cannot free ourselves. We confess that we have sinned against You in thought, word and deed, by what we have said and left unsaid, by what we have done and left undone. Forgive us Father and cleanse us!

Have mercy on our city! Forgive us for unlawful business deals, bribery, bloodshed, illegal gains, unjust weights, immoral businesses, and for not caring for the widows and orphans.

We release and forgive all those who have caused destruction in the city. We release city officials, business people, religious leaders, school personnel, parents and children. We release and forgive!

Father, forgive us and help us to operate in unity and love with one purpose which is to bring Your Kingdom to our city.

5. Lead Us Not Into Temptation, But Deliver Us From Evil

We appropriate Your name and promises over this city.

Sin will not reign in this city because You have set the watchman and gatekeepers of the city. You have given eyes to see the fiery darts of the enemy and You have given strength to stand in the gap and declare Your word, Your standard and Your will to be done in the city.

We have prepared in Your boot camp and we are ready to put on Your whole armor and declare we are strong in the Lord and in the power of Your might!

We speak in the name of the Lord to the enemies of our city government, of our precincts, of our churches, of our neighborhoods, of our schools and of our families:
We say to you enemy in the power and authority of the name of Jesus – GIVE UP THE LOST SOULS! We have come in the authority of Jesus to take back what belongs to Him! GIVE THEM UP! GIVE THEM UP! GIVE THEM UP NOW, AND YOU GET OUT OF THIS CITY!

By the authority of Jesus Christ, we decree and declare that souls will be added daily to the body of Christ, and we ask for the release of angels to minister to the heirs of salvation!

In the name of Jesus, we declare war on the enemy of our city! We wrestle not against flesh and blood, but against the rulers of darkness of the age, against spiritual hosts of wickedness in heavenly places.

Under the power and authority of Jesus Christ, we step into the enemy camp and take back what belongs to Jesus Christ!

We take dominion of the city under the same power and authority! In the name of Jesus, we bind the strongman and render him useless and ineffective over our city!

In the authority of Jesus, we take authority over demonic spirits that are controlling the spirits, souls and bodies of the citizens of our city!

We say to you enemy, we see your schemes with the citizens of our city and we declare to you that we are servants of the most High God, and we walk in His power and authority. We declare you powerless in the lives of God's servants in this city and we declare to you in His name that the lost souls in this city are covered by the Blood of Jesus for protection from you.

We know the Blood of Jesus will never lose its power. It reaches to the mountaintops and flows to the lowest valley. His Blood gives us strength for battle and we stand in the position of victor for this city.

In the power and authority of the name of Jesus given to us to pray in His will, we pray that the spirits of spiritualism, witchcraft and false religions be bound in our city. We pray that their words be confusing and ineffective. We pray that their be a loosening of praise over praise in our city and that Your truth permeate the innermost parts of our citizens.

In Your name Jesus, we ask that You bind the spirits that torment the souls of our city - spirits of depression, low self-esteem, oppression, rejection, suicide, anger, murder, jealousy, poverty, fear and malice.

We ask in Your name Jesus that You loose on our citizens faith, hope, love, joy, peace, patience, goodness, kindness, gentleness, sound minds, self-control, acceptance, and the mind of Christ.

We ask that You bind all demonic acts against the physical body, such as, lust, sexual perversions, adultery, homosexuality, lesbianism, child abuse child abandonment, child endangerment, molestation, wife abuse, domestic violence, drug addiction, alcoholism and all physical maladies.

Lord Jesus, in the power and authority of Your name and in Your will, we ask that You loose healing, strong families, purity of the body, favor, grace, wisdom, protection, miracles, friendships, assurance, strength and power to stand.

We pray that You will place a hedge of protection around our city. We thank You for Your protection and we know You have dispatched guardian angels to encamp around out cities, our schools, our churches and our homes, guardian angels who war for our city in the heavenly places.

6. For Thine Is The Kingdom And The Power And The Glory Forever.

We thank You Father that Your Kingdom reigns Supreme in the hearts of Your people in our city. We praise Your power and might Lord. We are strong in You and in the power of Your might. We thank You, and we declare, and see, Your glory coming down on our city. We praise Your name, for You reign in majesty over this city.

To You O' Lord be the glory and power forever.
AMEN

Ephesians 4:11-13 (NLT)

He is the one who gave these gifts to the church: the apostles, the prophets, the evangelists, and the pastors and teachers. [12]Their responsibility is to equip God's people to do his work and build up the church, the body of Christ, [13]until we come to such unity in our faith and knowledge of God's Son that we will be mature and full grown in the Lord, measuring up to the full stature of Christ.

APPENDIX 4

Sample Tabernacle Prayer

The Brazen Alter

1. Thank you for Your Blood to forgive all my sins.

2. I confess that I am a sinner and have sinned against You in thought, word and deed. I confess .....(Specific sins) ... ask Jesus to show you areas of your life needing to be confessed and repented of.

3. I crucify myself, my sinful, natural man, my flesh. I place myself on the cross with You.

4. I worship You because through Your Blood You have delivered me from the power of Satan and of the world.

5. Through Your strips I am healed and I praise you for divine healing through Your Blood.

6. I praise You for freeing me from the curse of Adam because of his sin. You took that curse to the cross.

7. Your Word says You have redeemed me from the law and that I am delivered from failure and poverty caused by the fall of Adam.

8. Through Your Blood I am delivered from death and hell. You conquered death and hell. By your Blood I am completely delivered from death and hell and am now living in Your Glory and am a member of the kingdom of God.

The Laver

1. Oh God, make me righteous through Your grace.

2. Heavenly Father, cleanse me from all unrighteousness.

3. Father, put in me a clean heart. A heart that is pleasing to You.

4. Increase my faithfulness to You.

5. Make me faithful and loyal to You Father, especially as far as Your 10 Commandments are concerned.

6. Oh God, purify me, sanctify me, and make me holy so I will be pleasing in Your sight.

7. Sanctify me in Your power.

8. Father, give me Your grace so that I may forgive ....

9. Holy Father, You help me to forgive ...., please also help me to love them.

10. Father God, I know you cleanse me and forgive me, please help me to have a very soft and loving heart to my brothers, sisters and neighbors.

11. Heavenly Father, help me to live according to the

measure of faith that You give me. Keep me from pride and from the evil one and to live each moment according to the fullness of the faith you have given to me.

Golden Candlestick

1. Dear Holy Spirit, I recognize You. I welcome You. I love and adore You.

2. Thank You Holy Spirit for being in my life.

3. You are the Spirit of God and Jesus

4. You are the Spirit of wisdom

5. You are the Spirit of understanding.

6. You are the Spirit of counsel.

7. You are the Spirit of power.

8. You are the Spirit of revelation of the Word of God.

9. You are the Spirit of the fear of God or of reverence, which gives me the power to reveal God to others.

10. Holy Spirit, I ask you to help me now. I cannot do anything without Your anointing. I depend on You. I worship You. I thank You. I love You. I admire You. I depend upon You. I can't handle the situations in my life and I depend upon You, please come with me.

The Table of Shewbread

1. Lord, your fresh shewbread is placed on the table

each day. It is Your fresh Word each day.

2. Lord, I admire and love the Word of God. I long after the Word of God.

3. Heavenly Father, help me to read, study, believe your fresh Word each day.

4. Lord, give me a new, fresh revelation in my heart today from Your Word.

5. My heart is panting for the Word of God so open my mind and my heart to your revelation today.

The Altar of Incense

1. I sing praises to You. I pray and sing to you in the special prayer language you gave me. Please accept the praises of Your saint.

2. I love you and give all praise and glory to You. You delivered me from sin. You delivered me from worldliness. You delivered me from sickness. You delivered me from the curse. You delivered me form death. You are the God who is the foundation of my life. You are the value of my life.

3. I worship You, the God who created the heavens and the earth and all things in them.

4. I love you with every part of my being and I sing praises to You.

Ark of the Covenant

1. Heavenly Father, when Jesus died on the cross You opened up the Holy of Holies by tearing the

curtain from top to bottom so I could come in through the shed Blood of Jesus Christ.

2. I see Your Ark of the Covenant Father and know that the three items You had placed there represent Your supernatural presence. In Your Ark is the rod of Aaron, which supernaturally budded; the tablets of law, which You supernaturally engraved; the manna, which You supernaturally provided in the wilderness for Your people.

3. I enter into the Holy of Holies and run to the Mercy Seat on top of Your Ark of the Covenant and I see Your Shekinah glory. I see the throne of God. I see the Ark of the Covenant.

4. I join You at Your mercy seat, in the Shekinah glory of Your presence, beneath the wings of the Cherubim.

5. Dear precious Heavenly Father, I am in awe at Your supernatural presence. I could not be more humbled then I am by Your presence.

6. I love You. I worship You. I adore You.

7. Father, I know I am eternally forgiven. I am eternally declared righteous. I am eternally saved. I am eternally blessed by the Blood covenant of Jesus Christ.

8. Thank You Heavenly Father, I know I am in Your Family. I know I am a child of Yours. I know I am living in the Holy of Holies.

9. Now Father, I have many requests and I ask You to hear them. I will only ask what is Your will and promises; I will ask only so You will be glorified and not myself or anyone else.

Psalm 2: 4-6 (NLT)

But the one who rules in heaven laughs. The Lord scoffs at them. ⁵Then in anger he rebukes them, terrifying them with his fierce fury. ⁶For the LORD declares, "I have placed my chosen king on the throne in Jerusalem, my holy city."

Psalm 114:7 (NLT)

Tremble, O earth, at the presence of the Lord, at the presence of the God of Israel.

Colossians 1:22 (NLT)

Yet now He has brought you back as his friends. He has done this through his death on the cross in His own human body. As a result, He has brought you into the very presence of God, and you are holy and blameless as you stand before Him without a single fault.

Suggested Reading

Nehemiah 2:17-18 (NLT)

But now I said to them, "You know full well the tragedy of our city. It lies in ruins, and its gates are burned. Let us rebuild the wall of Jerusalem and rid ourselves of this disgrace!" 18Then I told them about how the gracious hand of God had been on me, and about my conversation with the king.

They replied at once, "Good! Let's rebuild the wall!" So they began the good work.

SUGGESTED READING

Aldrich, Joe. **Reunitus.** (Sisters, OR: Multnomah Press, 1992).

Arnold, Clinton. **Powers of Darkness.** (Downers Grove, IL: Intervarsity Press, 1992)

Bakke, Ray. **A Theology as Big as the City**. (Downers Grove: InterVarsity Press, 1997)

Bernard, Daniel. **City Impact.** (Grand Rapids, MI: Chosen Books, 2004)

Bryant, David. **Christ is All.** (New Providence, NJ: Hew Providence Publishers, Inc., 2004)

Barna, George. **The Power of Vision.** (Ventura, CA: Regal Books,1992)

_____. **Evangelism That Works.** (Ventura, CA: Regal Books, 1995

_____. **The Second Coming of the Church.** (Nashville, TN: World Publishing, 1998)

_____. **Re-churching the Unchurched.** (Ventura, CA: Issachar Resources, 2000)

_____. **Boiling Point.** (Ventura, CA: Regal Books, 2001)

Beckett, Bob. **Commitment to Conquer.** (Grand Rapids, MI: Chosen Books, 1997).

Chrislip, David and Carl Larson. **Collaborative Leadership**. (San Francisco: Jossey- Bass, 1994)

Damazio, Frank. **The Gate Church.** (Portland, OR: City Bible Publishing, 2000)

Dawson, John. **Taking Our Cities for God.** (Lake Mary, FL: Creation House, 1989).

_____. **Healing America's Wounds.** (Ventura, CA: Regal Books, 1994)

Dennison, Jack. **City Reaching.** (Pasadena, CA: William Carey Library, 1999)

Frangipane, Francis. **The House of the Lord.** (Lake Mary, FL: Creation House, 1991)

Gladwell, Malcolm. **The Tipping Point.** (Boston: Little Brown, 2000)

Haggard, Ted. **Primary Purpose**. (Lake Mary, FL: Creation House, 1995)

_____. **Taking It To The Streets.** (Colorado Springs, CO: Wagner Publications, 2002)

Haggard, Ted and Jack Hayford. **Loving Your City into the Kingdom**. (Ventura, CA: Regal/Gospel Light, 1997)

Herrington, Jim, James Furr and Mike Bonem. **Leading Congregational Change** (San Francisco:Jossey-Bass Publishers, 1999)

Koivisto, Rex. **One Faith, One Body.** (Wheaton: Bridgepoint, 1993)

Layton, Douglas. **Our Father's Kingdom: The Church and the Nations** (Nashville TN: World Impact Press, 2000)

_____. **One Lord, One Faith**. (Wheaton: Bridgepoint, 1993)

Linthicum, Robert. **City of God City of Satan: A Biblical Theology of the Urban Church.** (Grand Rapids: Zondervan Publishing House, 1991)

Lean, Garth. **God's Politician: William Wilberforce's Struggle**. (London: Darton, Longman and Todd, 1980)

Nathan, Rich and Ken Wilson. **Empowered Evangelicals**. (Ann Arbor: Servant Publications, 1995)

Marshall, Rich **God @ Work.** (Shippensburg, PA: Destiny Image, 2000)

Otis, Jr., George. **The Last of the Giants.** (Grand Rapids, MI: Chosen Books, 1991)

_____. **The Twilight Labyrinth.** (Grand Rapids, MI: Chosen Books, 1997)

_____. **Informed Intercession.** (Ventura, CA: Renew/Gospel Light, 1999)

_____. **God's Trademarks.** (Grand Rapids, MI: Chosen Books, 2000)

Pier, Mac and Sweeting, Kathy. **The Power of a City at Prayer – What Happens When Churches Unite for Renewal.** (Downers Grove, Il: InterVasity Press, 2002)

Pierce, Chuck and Rebecca Wagner Sytsema. **The Future War of the Church.** (Ventura, CA: Regal Books, 2001)

Ruibal, Ruth. **Unity in the Spirit.** (Lynnwood, WA: Transformnations Media, 2002)

Sheets, Dutch. **Intercessory Prayer.** (Ventura, CA:

Regal Books, 1996)

_____. **Watchman Prayer.** (Ventura, CA: Regal Books, 2000)

Sherratt, Timothy and Ronald Mahurn. **Saints as Citizens** (Grand Rapids: Baker Books, 1995)

Silvoso, Ed. **Anointed for Business.** (Ventura, CA: Regal, 2002)

_____. **Prayer Evangelism.** (Ventura, CA: Regal, 2000)

_____. **That None Should Perish.** (Ventura, CA: Regal Books, 1994)

Smith, Timothy. **Revivalism and Social Reform.** (New York: Harper and Row, 1965)

Stringer, Doug. **Somebody Cares...A Guide to Living Out Your Faith.** (Ventura: Regal/Gospel Light, 2001)

Tenney, Tommy. **The God Chasers.** (Shippensburg, PA: Destiny Image Publishers, Inc., 1999)

_____. **God's Dream Team.** (Ventura, CA: Regal Books, 1999)

Wagner, C. Peter. **Breaking Strongholds In Your City.** (Ventura, CA: Regal Books, 1993)

_____. **Radical Holiness for Radical Living.** (Colorado Springs, CO: Wagner Publications, 1998)

_____. **Revival! It Can Transform Your City.** (Colorado Springs, CO: Wagner Publications, 1999)

_____. **Apostles of the City.** (Colorado Springs, CO: Wagner Publications, 2000)

Warren, Rick. **The Purpose Driven Church.** (Grand Rapids: Zondervan Publishing House, 1995)

Waymire, Bob and Carl Townsend. **Discovering Your City.** (Etna, CA: Light International, 2000)

White, Randy. **Journey to the Center of the City – Making a Difference in an Urban Neighborhood.** (Downers Grove, Il: InterVasity Press, 1996)

White, Tom. **City-Wide Prayer Movements.** (Ann Arbor, MI: Servant Publications, 2001).

Proverbs 11:10-11 (NLT)

The whole city celebrates when the godly succeed; they shout for joy when the godless die.

[11]Upright citizens bless a city and make it prosper, but the talk of the wicked tears it apart.

Proverbs 16:32 (NLT)

It is better to be patient than powerful; it is better to have self-control than to conguer a city.

Index

Ephesians 2:20-22 (NLT)

We are his house, built on the foundation of the apostles and the prophets. And the cornerstone is Christ Jesus himself. [21] We who believe are carefully joined together, becoming a holy temple for the Lord. [22] Through him you Gentiles are also joined together as part of this dwelling where God lives by his Spirit.

INDEX

D

E

F

G

S

T

Services Offered

Jeremiah 9:23-24

This is what the LORD says: "Let not the wise man gloat in his wisdom, or the mighty man in his might, or the rich man in his riches. 24Let them boast in this alone: that they truly know me and understand that I am the LORD who is just and righteous, whose love is unfailing, and that I delight in these things. I, the LORD, have spoken!

SERVICES OFFERED

By
Rev. Dr. D. Vincent (Bud) Ford
The Dwelling Place Ministries, Inc.
Author of
Transformation: The Missing Piece

I am able to hold two to five-day revival meetings, seminars, workshops or teach on many topics related to reaching cities.

If you are interested in talking, you can email me at budford@bright.net or call 937-492-7633 and we can arrange a time to talk.

Available to preach, teach, hold revival services, seminars or workshops on the following:
1. The Tabernacle model for the presence of God
2. The Seven Churches in Revelation
3. Christ's message to us from the book of Revelation (A message of Hope)
4. Going outside the four walls of the church
5. Walking in the Spirit
6. Prayer
7. Faith
8. Deliverance
9. Healing
10. Revival
11. TRANSFORMATION: The Missing Piece
12. Topics on bringing people into the presence of God through the Tabernacle pattern
13. Marion Correction Institution Model for TRANSFORMATION

14. City reaching
15. TRANSFORMATION: The Missing Piece
16. Outreach—Neighborhood Prayer saturation and follow-up
17. Prayer Fairs in neighborhoods
18. Freeing workers for the harvest (providing instruction and opportunities to practice is the best way to prepare Harvest Workers)
19. Marion Correctional Institution—TRANSFORMATION
20. Information on Free Masonry (as an ex-Mason, Shriner and Scottish Rite member)
21. Redemptive Gifts
    a. Of Individuals
    b. Of Cities
    c. Principles, Bondages, Strongholds, Blessings and Curses
22. Meeting with cross denominational/racial leadership on vision and strategy
23. Meeting with individual church leadership that desires unity of the Body of Christ
24. TRANSFORMATION: The Missing Piece
25. Prayer Walking
26. Lighthouses of Prayer

CONTACT INFORMATION:

Dr. D. Vincent (Bud) Ford
718 Stratford Dr.
Sidney Ohio 45365
budford@bright.net
937-492-7633
1-800-936-3599
www.DrBudFord.com
www.DVincentFord.com
www.TheDwellingPlaceMinistries.com
www.TransformationTheMissingPiece.com

Romans 12:1-2 (NLT)

And so, dear brothers and sisters, I plead with you to give your bodies to God. Let them be a living and holy sacrifice—the kind he will accept. When you think of what he has done for you, is this too much to ask? ²Don't copy the behavior and customs of this world, but let God transform you into a new person by changing the way you think. Then you will know what God wants you to do, and you will know how good and pleasing and perfect his will really is.

James 2:17 (NLT)

So you see, it isn't enough just to have faith. Faith that doesn't show itself by good deeds is no faith at all—it is dead and useless.

ABOUT THE AUTHOR

Dr. Ford has been involved in city transformation efforts for the past twelve years and his qualifications include the following:

- Ph.D. received from Ohio University,
- Public high school social studies teacher for four years
- Front line public high school principal for sixteen years
- Christian school superintendent for seven years
- Ordained Clergy with Seminary studies completed from Berean University
- Assistant pastor for one year
- Ministry founder of the 501-C-3 non-profit corporation The Dwelling Place Ministries, Inc. which is dedicated to transforming America, city by city in this generation.

In his role as president of The Dwelling Place Ministries, Dr. Ford has facilitated pastors' groups, led outreach, organized pastors' summits, led community-wide task forces, chaired community committees and participated in city-reachers schools, seminars and conferences to numerous to mention.

Dr. Ford is a popular speaker in churches and he has conducted numerous workshops and seminars.

Contact Information:
D. Vincent Ford, The Dwelling Place Ministries
718 Stratford Dr., Sidney, Ohio 45365-1948
1-937-492-7633 & 1-800-936-3599
www.DrBudFord.com
www.DVincentFord.com
www.TransformationTheMissingPiece.com

1 John 4:2-3 (NLT)
This is the way to find out if they have the Spirit of God: If a prophet acknowledges that Jesus Christ became a human being, that person has the Spirit of God. If a prophet does not acknowledge Jesus, that person is not from God. Such a person has the spirit of the Antichrist. You have heard that he is going to come into the world, and he is already here.

POSTAGE AND HANDLING RATES
Call for UPS Next Day Air® rates

STANDARD SHIPPING	UPS GROUND®	PRIORITY MAIL	UPS 2ND DAY AIR®
Up to $20 $3.50	Up to $20—$5.50	Up to $20—$9.50	Up to $20—$9.50
20.01 - 50 5.00	20.01 - 50 7.50	20.01 - 50 11.00	20.01 - 50 11.00
50.01 - 100. 10%	50.01 - 100 15%	50.01 - 100 22%	50.01 - 100 22%
100.01 & Up 8%	100.01 & Up 12%	100.01 & Up 18%	100.01 & Up 18%
Estimated delivery time 1 to 2 weeks. Generally delivered via U.S. Postal Service. May be delivered by multiple carriers. APO & FPO customers may add $1.75 for PAL shipment.	Delivery time 1 to 6 business days. Available in the contiguous U.S. only. Street address required.	Delivery time 2 to 6 business days. For use to P.O. Box, AK, HI, APO/FPO, and U.S. Protectorates. Valid UPS addresses will be shipped UPS 2nd Day Air.	Delivery time 1 to 2 Business days. Available in the contiguous U.S. only. Street address required.

Shipping time frames are contingent upon when your order has been received and processed. Charges are for each address we ship to. Orders shipped to AK, HI, APO/FPO. and U.S. Protectorates may require additional delivery dates.

CANADIAN AND OVERSEAS SHIPMENT	
Canada	**Economy Air Service** (2-6 weeks delivery)
Up to $30 7.50	Up to $30 10.00
30.01 - 200. 25%	30.01 - 200. 35%
200.01 and Up 20%	200.01 & Up 30%

Order Form
TRANSFORMATION: THE MISSING PIECE

Please send me the following:

Quantity:	Item:	Price:
_____	Transformation: The Missing Piece	$16.95ea. _____
		Tax 6% _____

See Shipping & Handling rate on page 270 and list your preferred shipping cost. The rates pertain to the Book retail prices only.	Shipping & Handling per book within USA _____
	TOTAL _____

Customer Information (please print)

Name:_____

Mailing Address:_____

City:_____State:_____ZIP:_____

Phone:_____

Fax:_____

email:_____

Make check payable to: Streams Publishing Co.

BOOK ORDERING INFORMATION
Mail Order Form to:
Streams Publishing Company
Dr. D. Vincent (Bud) Ford
718 Stratford Dr., Sidney, OH 45365-1948
OR
FAX Order Form with Credit Card number and experation date to: 1-937-492-7633
OR
Call Toll FREE to 1-800-936-3599 and have your Credit Card information ready
OR
Order online at www.TransformationTheMissingPiece.com
www.DrBudFord.com

2 Corinthians 5:15-21 (NLT)

He died for everyone so that those who receive his new life will no longer live to please themselves. Instead, they will live to please Christ, who died and was raised for them.

[16]So we have stopped evaluating others by what the world thinks about them. Once I mistakenly thought of Christ that way, as though he were merely a human being. How differently I think about him now. [17]What this means is that those who become Christians become new persons. They are not the same anymore, for the old life is gone. A new life has begun!

[18]All this newness of life is from God, who brought us back to himself throughwhat Christ did. And God has given us the task of reconciling people to him. [19]For God was in Christ, reconciling the world to himself, no longer counting people's sins against them. This is the wonderful message he has given us to tell others. [20]We are Christ's ambassadors, and God is using us to speak to you. We urge you, as though Christ himself were here pleading with you, "Be reconciled to God!" [21]For God made Christ, who never sinned, to be the offering for our sin, so that we could be made right with God through Christ.

Order Form
Transformation: The Missing Piece

Please send me the following:

Quantity:	Item:	Price:	
_____	Transformation: The Missing Piece	$16.95ea. Tax 6%	_____ _____

See Shipping & Handling rate on page 270 and list your preferred shipping cost. The rates pertain to the Book retail prices only.	Shipping & Handling per book within USA	_____
	TOTAL	_____

Customer Information (please print)

Name:_____

Mailing Address:_____

City:_____State:____ZIP:_____

Phone:_____

Fax:_____

email:_____

Make check payable to: Streams Publishing Co.

BOOK ORDERING INFORMATION
Mail Order Form to:
Streams Publishing Company
Dr. D. Vincent (Bud) Ford
718 Stratford Dr., Sidney, OH 45365-1948
OR
FAX Order Form with Credit Card number and experation date to: 1-937-492-7633
OR
Call Toll FREE to 1-800-936-3599 and have your Credit Card information ready
OR
Order online at www.TransformationTheMissingPiece.com
www.DrBudFord.com

Proverb 29:23 (NLT)
Pride ends in humiliation, while humility brings honor.